AF473724

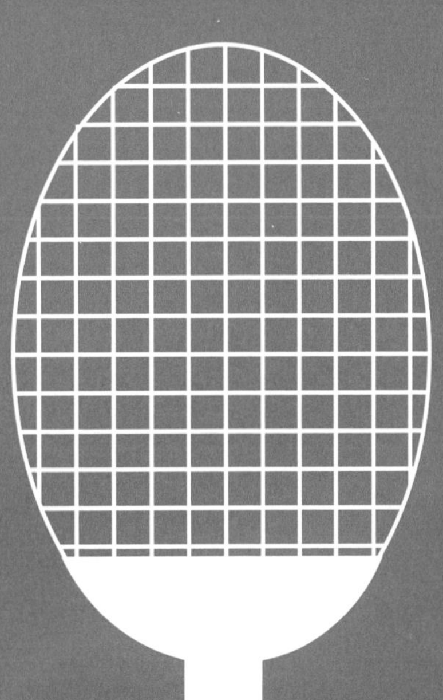

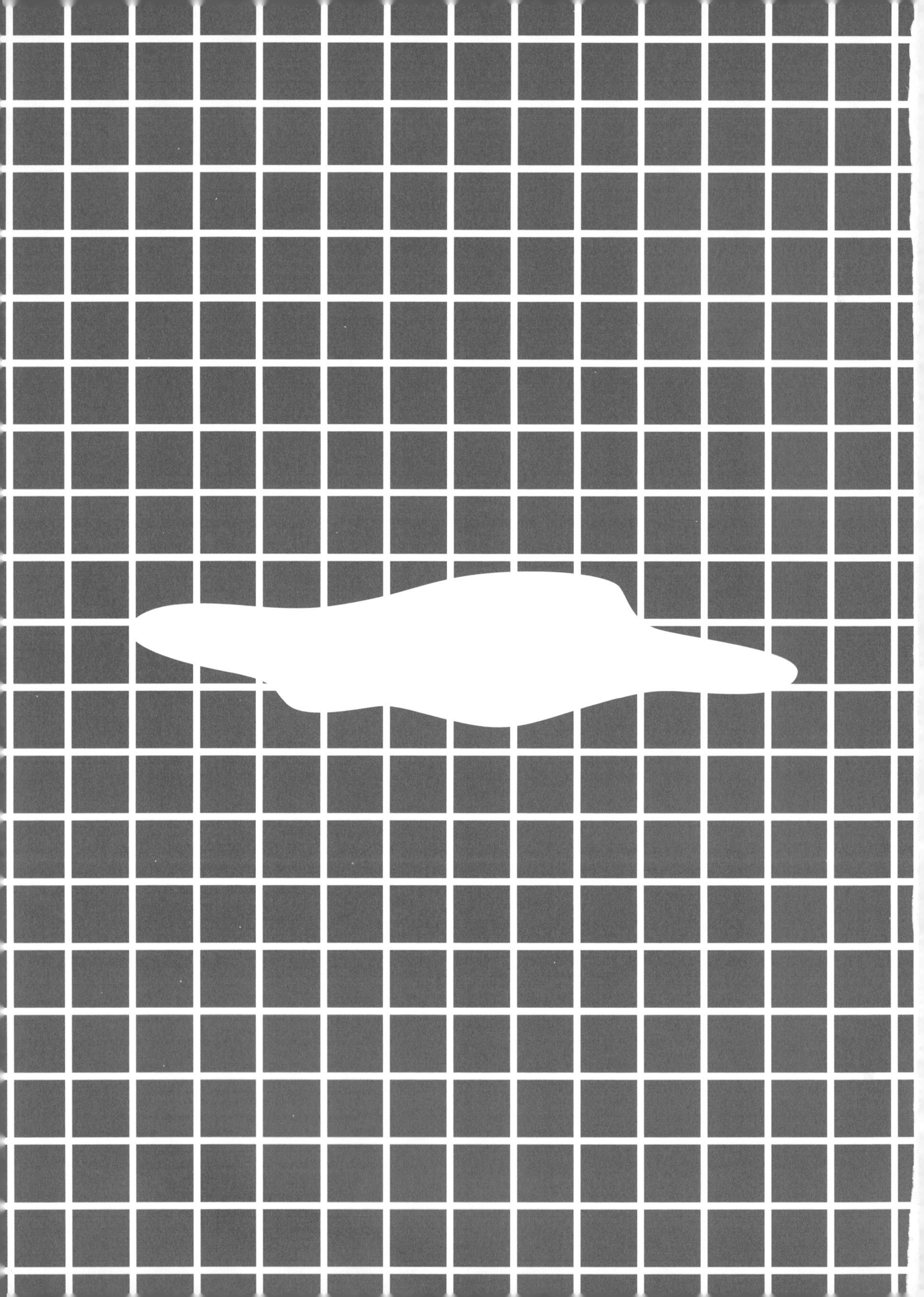

JAPANESE ILLUSTRATION

sendpoints

CONTENTS

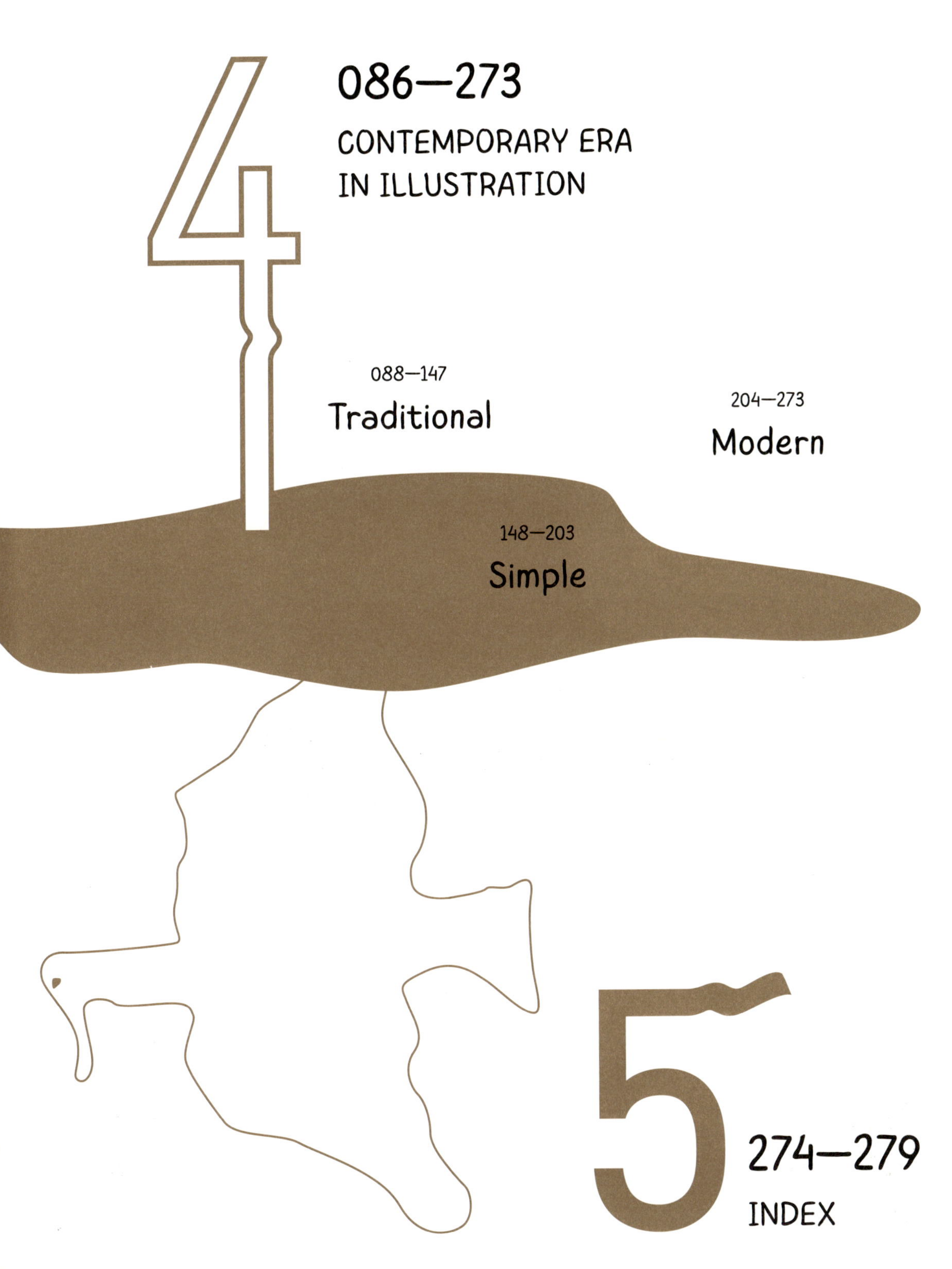

加藤直＝作 村松克己＝演出
シュールレアリズム宣言
おや、あれはもしかしたら二十世紀文明！
平山戯るか？ 殺るか？ ドキマギするか？
くすぐられる裸美人と喰われる名探偵
恍惚を 笑いの極限で
リアリズムする 徹底的爆笑涙々篇
最後の吸血鬼の
トランシルバニアの
天駆ける蒼穹のなかへ
黒色テントが
さらわれて
しまう！
68/71
同時上演
百連発
堀田正彦＝作 津野海太郎＝演出

Preface

JAPANESE ILLUSTRATION IN DESIGN HISTORY

Chapter 1

When youngsters chasing after the "minimalist style" begin sharing a wide variety of costumes and accessories bought from MUJI and UNIQLO, when Xiaomi's new logo designed by Kenya Hara became a new topic of joke writers, and when the mini version of the new iPhone again triggers the nostalgia for the "times of Jobs," we raise one after another question in the multifarious but haphazard urban views: "What is design? What is the design of beauty? How should the language of design combine art and life?"

Shigeru Uchida, a famous Japanese design master, believes that design should be people-oriented. Similarly, graphic design master Kenya Hara pointed out that the greatest power of design awakening. The value of design in life is to provide people with creative motivation and demand.

In modernization development, the aesthetics and methodology of Japanese design have always been featured by spiritual precipitation that cannot be simply imitated by the West. The tacit agreement in terms of color between the porcelain of the 1950s and the trendy boutique stores of the 21st century means that the Japanese tradition contains the aesthetics of life. Generations of Japanese designers have tapped into the value of traditional culture to constantly create and explore new charm.

01

01. ***Sakurajima, Kagoshima,* from the series *Selected Views of Japan***

Hasui Kawase, 1922

Source: Wikimedia

02. ***Flower Basket Painting***

Ogata Kenzan, the Edo Period, Fukuoka Art Museum

Source: Wikimedia

03. ***Teabowl with Moonflower (Yūgao) and Poem***

Ogata Kenzan, the 18th century

Source: Wikimedia

There has been a fusion between design, art, and life. The minute details of everyday life offer a glimpse into the origin of human life and present their purity to be sources of beauty we can draw. Calligraphy and drawing are combined. The Mon (Japanese emblems used to decorate and identify an individual, a family, an institution, or a business entity) and Ukiyo-e are integrated into people's daily life. Scrolls and screens become indispensable decorations in living space. The drawing nature has been reflected in the daily life of Japanese people. Throughout history, humans have used narrative images to tell stories. The earliest recorded illustrations appear in cave paintings at Lascaux, France, about 15,000 years ago. Illustration is derived from the Latin term "*illustratio*," which means "to illuminate." In other words, illustrations are able to make the text and its information clearer and enhance their interest and vividness. The art of illustration features a time-honored history. From cave

02

03

04. *Fukagawa Susaki and Jumantsubo*, from the series *One Hundred Famous Views of Edo*

Utagawa Hiroshige, 1857, Collection of the Tokyo Fuji Art Museum

Source: Wikimedia

05. *A Thousand Cranes*

Matazo Kayama, 1970, Collection of the National Museum of Modern Art, Tokyo

Source: Wikimedia

paintings to Ukiyo-e, the art of illustration continues to develop and is widely used in all fields of design.

Japanese design spirit and design concept are not only the result of design thinking but also a deep understanding of the philosophy of life. However, where does Japanese design come from?

First, Japan is a country that values beauty. Streets, temples, flowers, branches, waterfronts, and other elements all present the nation's aesthetic thought, which also are embodied in the works of Japanese decorated drawing school. Rinpa founded by Hon'ami Koetsu and Tawaraya Sotatsu, fully amassed and established by Ogata Korin and Ogata Kenzan, and finally inherited and developed by Ito Jakuchu, Sakai Hoitsu, Matazo Kayama, and others, has become a classic model of Japanese art and has had a profound influence on Japanese plastic arts. Rinpa paintings are mainly screen drawings and involve many craft areas such as costumes, lacquerware, pottery, and others. Screens, which are related to Japanese architectural styles, are decorative objects and artifacts in their own right. Since then, the beauty of daily objects has added a splendid touch to Japanese design.

Ikko Tanaka, a leading figure in Japanese graphic design after the 1950s, has presented his designs based on the Rinpa School. He was honored at the New York Art Directors Club Hall of Fame in 1994. He called the Rinpa School the prototype of the "physical look of Japan."

05

06

春乃夕
（上野東照宮）

08

In Ikko Tanaka's description, it is an elegant, free, open-minded and gorgeous world. It does not boast of its own beauty, but shows a warm world as if basked in the early spring sunshine and eulogizes the wonderful flavor of the four seasons in Japan.

Second, Japanese design is deeply influenced by the world around it. During the Edo Period (1603—1867), Japan's economy and culture flourished, as did

06. ***Autumn at Okuirise***

Hasui Kawase, 1933

07. ***Spring Dusk at the Toshogu Shrine, Ueno***

Hasui Kawase, 1948

08. ***The Amida Falls in the Far Reaches of the Kiso Road*****, from the series *A Tour of Waterfalls in Various Provinces***

Katsushika Hokusai, 1833, Museum of Fine Arts, Boston, William Sturgis Bigelow Collection

Source: Wikimedia

09. ***Asakusa Ricefields and Torinomachi Festival*****, from the series *One Hundred Famous Views of Edo***

Utagawa Hiroshige, 1857—1858, Collection of the Tokyo National Museum

Source: Wikimedia

09

design and creativity. Ukiyo-e, as a significant school of woodblock print and drawing in Japan, developed during this period. Traditional Ukiyo-e absorbed the techniques of Chinese engraving in the Ming (1368-1644) and Qing (1644-1912) Dynasties. It was based on manually made paintings and woodblock prints, distinguishly represented by woodblock prints that could be reproduced in large quantities. Ukiyo-e mainly depicts people's daily life, scenery, and dramas, vividly showing the various social situations and customs of that era. It has been known as the "encyclopedia" of folk customs of the Edo Period.

10

11

10. ***The Great Wave off Kanagawa*** **from the series *Thirty-Six Views of Mount Fuji***

Katsushika Hokusai, 1831

11. ***Fine Wind, Clear Morning*** **from the series *Thirty-Six Views of Mount Fuji***

Katsushika Hokusai, 1830—1831, Collection of the Museum of Fine Arts, Boston

Source: Wikimedia

12. ***Nezumi Kozo: The Rat (4)***

Kouga Hirano, 1968—1971

Katsushika Hokusai, the "father of modern Japanese art," touched millions of people with his realistic style and delicate brushwork.

He was not only good at fine brushwork, but also good at freehand brushwork. His painting subject matters are highly rich, especially depicting the beautiful scenery of mountains and rivers in Japan and people's work life and hobbies. His representative work *The Great Wave off Kanagawa* is a masterpiece of traditional Japanese aesthetics and western techniques. The extraordinary line

12

黒色テントの胡蝶 新井純 山口美也子両嬢競艶!! 作・演出 佐藤信
the Hour of the Rat
お前はあの晩
腐った椿姫の死骸を抱いて
最后の「ある晴れた日に」を唄っていたのだったね 知っているよ――あの晩
お花畑は季節はずれの大雪で
遠くで
ささやかな叛乱の銃声が二、三発
そう それっきりさ――みんな
6871

symbol of Japanese Ukiyo-e. In its heyday, Ukiyo-e created "Japonism" in Europe, which influenced Impressionism, post-Impressionism, and Art Nouveau movements. To this day, Ukiyo-e continues to provide a source of inspiration for modern design. People can still borrow from Ukiyo-e's rich color schemes and aesthetic meanings when creating illustrations, comics, animations, and even electronic games.

During the Meiji Period (1868—1912), Japan opened up to the rest of the world and actively increased its exchanges with other countries in trade and culture including design. Western copperplates and oil paintings were introduced into Japan. The way of penetrating space and expressing the three-dimensional nature of things in paintings attracted many Japanese artists at that time. They began to imitate the use of Western oil colors in drawing, or integrate Western expression techniques into the Japanese tradition. Inspired by Western art and design, Japanese design creativity exploded.

14

After World War II, with the strong economic support of the United States, Japan's economy recovered and developed rapidly, enabling Japan to be the third largest economy in the world. Driven by postwar industrialization and manufacturing, industrial design techniques and concepts continued to expand. The style of constructivism and Bauhaus inspired Japanese design at that time. A large number of creations combining strong geometric shapes and Japanese symbolism fourished. During this period, Japanese design still paid attention to maintaining regional features, attached importance to historical inheritance, and integrated globalization with localization.

KOSHIMAKI-OSEN
腰巻お仙
路頭劇
状羅魔
MADE IN JAPAN
忘却編
作・唐十郎
劇団状況劇場第八回公演
戸山ハイツ灰かぐら劇場
十月二八↓三〇日夜八時
澁澤龍彦●日本の若い演劇界は百鬼夜行のありさまで、しかも西洋かぶれのチンピラの百鬼夜行だから、たまったものではない。そういう中で、唐十郎の存在は、たしかに異彩を放っている。
一陣の埃を巻きあげ、「状況劇場」が風のように駆け抜けたあとに、わたしは、ドラマツルギーの幻影が一瞬あらわれ、たちまちにして消え去るのを見る。唐十郎は、小出しに使う財産のようにドラマツルギーを持っているのではない。思想は実体があるはずはない。彼のドラマツルギーは、おそらく、「身命を山野に捨て、居住を風雲にまかせる」といった、鎌倉時代の無用者の心意気にも似た、言葉の真の意味における、河原乞食（すなわち役者）の行動哲学から由来するものであろう。少なくとも、彼はそれを目ざしているのであろう。
しかし、わたしの見た限り、「状況劇場」の芝居は、お伽草子の現代版のようにリリカルで、お祭の見世物のようにノスタルジックで、場末の衛生博覧会のように無気味である。胎児の恐怖、親なし子のさすらい、永遠のさすらい…
「状況劇場」もまた、古くてしかも新らしい、日本の土壌に生まれた親なし子のように、超前衛の道を永遠にさすらって行くことだろう。わたしはそれを期待している。
御存知
麿　赤児
吉沢　健
大久保　鷹
木田与之助
藤原マキ
李　礼仙
唐　十郎
連絡場所
844－4936
当日発売
A＝四〇〇円
M＝五〇〇円
Z＝八〇〇円
この人は唐十郎であります！
中国料理と西洋料理
お茶の水明大通り TEL 291－4024
招仙閣 SHOSEN KAKU
とんかつ・天ぷら
ときわ
お茶の水明大前
(291) 8759
現代に生きる古典音楽喫茶の殿堂！
名曲：珈琲
丘
DESIGN BY Tadanori Yokoo

13. *Snow, Moon and Flower: Snow, Asakusa Kinryuzan* (triptych)

Yasuji Inoue, 1885, Collection of the Artglorieux Gallery of Tokyo

14. *A View of American Prosperity*

Utagawa Hiroshige II, 1861

Source: Wikimedia

15. *Koshimaki-Osen*

Tadanori Yokoo, 1966, Collection of the MoMA

Source: Wikimedia

In the 1960s, the famous Japanese artist Tadanori Yokoo began to show his brilliant talents in Tokyo. Pop art swept the world at that time. Tadanori Yokoo attempted to combine Japanese folk customs and modern art in graphic design, giving birth to a series of popular works featuring rich colors, folk emotions, fantasy, and revelation of the spiritual world. Responding to the trend of the times, they were widely welcomed.

Starting from the Japanese traditional aesthetic taste and the folk "Mono no aware" aesthetics, Tadanori Yokoo goes beyond mechanically borrowing the Western Pop Art methodology in his artistic creation to display the retro folk customs highlighting the fresh texture, so as to reflect the real humanistic form of Japanese society.

In the 1990s, Japanese design exploded in an unprecedented way. With the development of postmodernism and computers, a whole new world of design has emerged. Japanese modern art has been given these characteristics: the "extraordinary skill" of the artisan spirit, the new expression born from the traditional culture, the perfect fusion of art and popular culture... Contemporary Japanese artists have brought us so many incredible impacts. The developed MAG (manga, anime, games) industry has enabled Japan to be hailed as the "land of two dimensions." The whole world marvels at Japan's imagination.

Based on its own national culture, Japanese design has formed a unique system and context in history and then influenced the whole world.

Reference:

1. *A History of Japanese Art*, written by Xu Xiaohu. Guangxi Normal University Press, 2019
2. *60 Years of Japanese Design*, written by Shigeru Uchida. CITIC Publishing House, 2018
3. *Illustrated History of Japanese Art*, written by Nobuo Tsuji (辻惟雄). SDX Joint Publishing Company, 2016

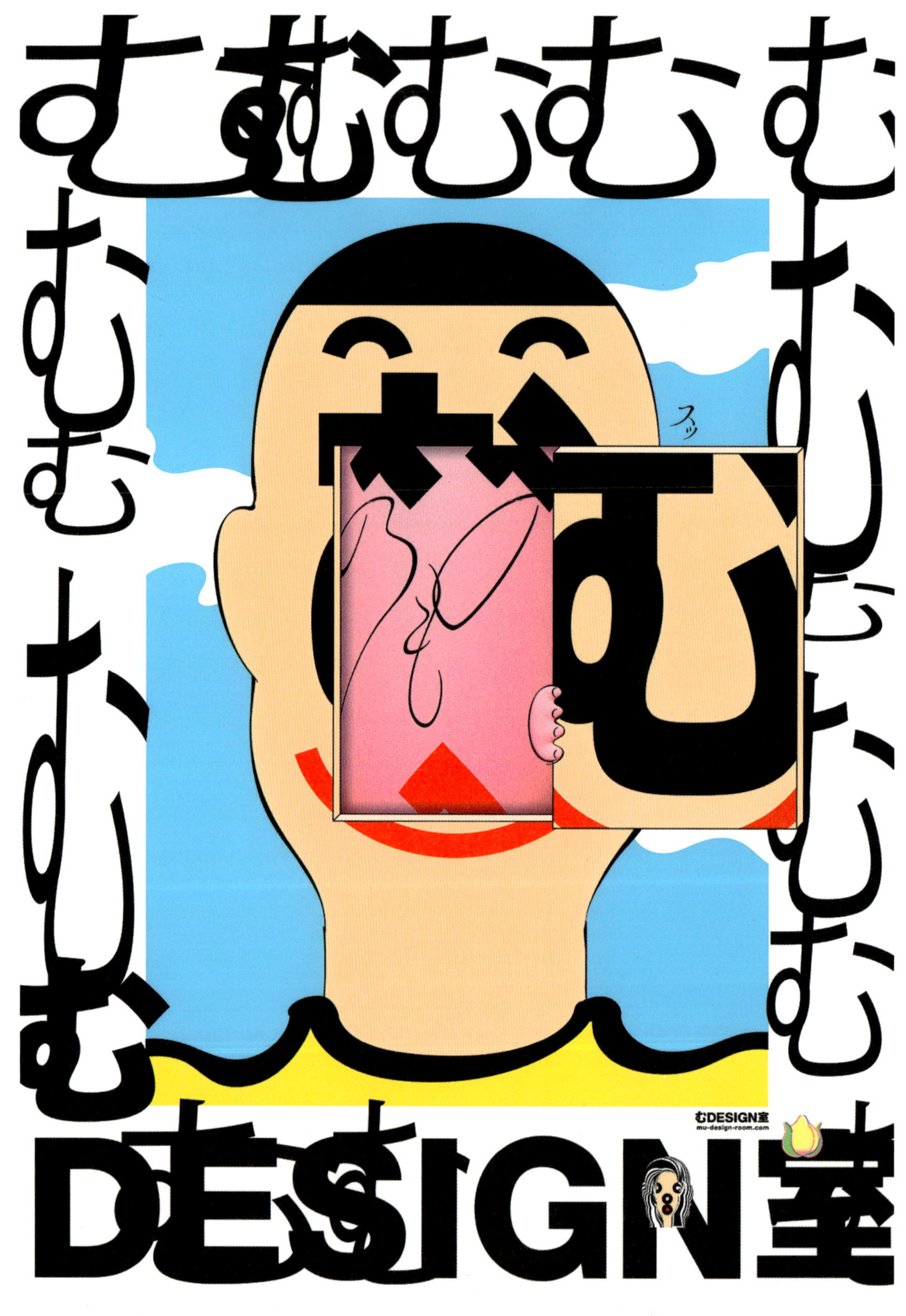

スッ
むDESIGN室
mu-design-room.com
DESIGN室

CREATIVITY IN ILLUSTRATION

Chapter

The design concept of Japan has been shaped by its special geographical location, historical periods, and unique social and cultural environment. While absorbing Western culture, Japanese design integrates the essence of their local folk customs, leaving unique impressions on people and permeating into people's daily life.

Spiritual precipitation also enables Japanese design to have the "exquisite and detailed expressive force," connecting the past, the present, and the future. Shigeru Uchida pointed out that design is to reproduce the ancient in the present; it is a job "to show the intangible future in tangible ways."

Oriental aesthetics and commercial culture have nourished the creativity of contemporary Japanese designers. In their respective extraordinary artistic careers, they associate with and analog from politics, economics, production, consumption, environment, and nature, thus contributing to intellectuality and diversity. "The flow of the river never ceases, and the water never stays the same. " (Kamo no Chōmei, Trans. Stavros, Matthew [2020]. *Hōjōki: A Hermit's Hut as Metaphor*, Kamo no Chomei). From the past to the future, the poetry and charm created by designers reverberate with the meanings and themes that emerge from the depths of their hearts.

This chapter takes the form of articles or interviews to converse with contemporary designers Shinnoske Sugisaki, Akiko Sekimoto, Hitoshi Akasako, Aoshi Kudo, Yasuhiro Sawada, Kazuo Kuribayashi, Takafumi Kusagaya, and Muramatsu Takehiko, to discuss their understanding of design and illustration, and to feel Japanese aesthetics in their eyes.

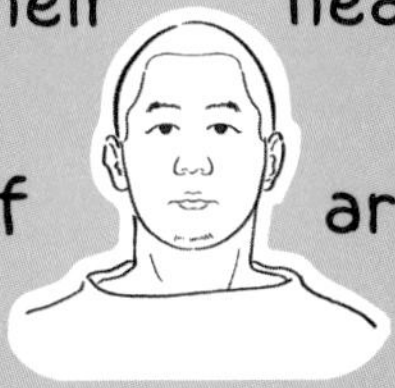

"The entirety of Japanese culture can be seen through the invisible 'filter'."

Shinnoske Sugisaki

Shinnoske Sugisaki

Creative Director of Shinnoske Design Inc., Professor of Osaka University of Arts, member of Alliance Graphique Internationale (AGI). Shinnoske Sugisaki views design as the construction of information and the planning of impressions, with the ultimate goal of clear and effective communication. He has worked on a wide range of projects, consistently applying design principles, spanning from cultural sectors to corporate branding, information design, and space graphics. He has exhibited and lectured in many places across the globe, actively presenting his experimental challenges. He has won a number of international awards, including ADC Special Awards, TDC Excellence Awards, HKDA Asian Design, and others. His works have been collected by many institutions such as the Museum für Kunst und Gewerbe Hamburg, the Hong Kong Heritage Museum, and others.

The aesthetics and spirit behind Japanese illustrations

From art to design and illustration, there are no boundaries in terms of expression; all are intended to "create joy." Having been engaged in design for more than 40 years, Shinnoske Sugisaki still believes in the necessity and possibility of design and maintains an understanding and tolerance of the world's diverse values. Although he is over 60 years old, Mr. Sugisaki maintains a bright heart and keeps creating. Upon thinking about many things he does not know about and has not yet discovered, he continues to learn from the design of the past and actively seek inspiration from the young artists of today.

To explore the aesthetics and spirit behind Japanese illustration, Shinnoske Sugisaki tried to capture the origins of illustration with the keywords "manga" and "printmaking." When it comes to "manga," Sugisaki believes that works represented by Animal-person Caricatures and Hokusai Manga have profoundly influenced the development of Japanese illustration. Both of them use "deformation," that is, to exaggerate and emphasize in order to simplify and express the features of the object. Later, "printmaking" appeared, giving rise to a large number of printed materials, which serve as carriers of arts. Thanks to the development of technology, Ukiyo-e, a multicolor wood print, has been able to spread from the early 17th century to modern times. From the Edo Period to the Meiji Period, a large number of printmaking works were spread among the Japanese people. It showed that Japanese art was not only found in elegant and gorgeous halls but also becoming a popular art in people's life. In modern times, illustrations spread through commodities, network media, and other carriers and ways.

Japanese aesthetics is deeply influenced by Western aesthetics. In Mr. Sugisaki's eyes, the expression form of Oriental visual art is a way of "overlooking the landscape from the perspective of nature." Its description of spatial depth presents multiple viewpoints to "flexibly express time and space," which also coincides with people's actual cognition of space. Oriental art is more used to depict things in outline, such as ink painting. More often than not, it uses colors and brightness that do not exist in nature to outline painted objects. Western visual art is more about "capturing the landscape from the perspective of people." Its description of spatial depth presents a single viewpoint, such as the "perspective drawing," which uses light and shadow to show painting objects. More often than not, it uses colors and brightness that do not exist in nature to show the outline of painting objects.

Like most people, the era Mr. Sugisaki grew up has deeply shaped his design career. He feels lucky to have spent his childhood and adolescence in times of great changes. In the 1950s, Mickey Mouse by Disney and Astro Boy by Osamu Tezuka swept Japanese society. By the 1960s, the American Push Pin Studios' fusion of illustration and graphic design, as well as its development in advertising and marketing, had a great deal of influence on the Japanese design field at the time. The Japanese illustration field subsequently developed. Around the 1970s, Mr. Sugisaki, then a college student, was deeply attracted by the artist Tadanori Yokoo, whose works were influenced by Ukiyo-e, pop art, and subculture, with strong color expression and all-encompassing values.

The development of manga and printmaking, and the interaction with European culture have promoted Japanese art. In contemporary Japanese society, in addition to traditional culture, there are distinctive manga and animation, and the post-modern otaku culture, which is vastly popular with young people. In the richer contemporary environment, the Japanese "wabi-sabi" philosophy system for objects is taken as the skeleton, supporting the fusion of more modern elements to show a richer artistic language. It also makes Japanese contemporary art go beyond the "traditional symbol" level and the imitation of the Western art language.

"The entirety of Japanese culture can be seen through the invisible 'filter'. " Mr. Sugisaki believes that Japanese aesthetic culture has nothing to do with the temporal, regional, and cultural context, but is more of a "mixed" refining process while foreign cultures constitute the nutrients of Japanese culture. Without external stimulus, Japan risks slipping into galapagosization[1]. On the other hand, Mr. Sugisaki argues that it is impossible to define Japanese aesthetics within a limited scope. If Japan is the "interior" and the world surrounding around Japan is the "exterior," then the "interior" and "exterior" will serve as a spiritual consciousness to form the mixed "Japanese style," presenting the minimalism such as "wabi-sabi." For example, the pop trend represented by the popular culture is diverse and extensive.

Contemporary illustration is deeply influenced and guided by commercial culture. In Mr. Sugisaki's opinion, illustrations that meet the needs of commercial design first require the illustrator to have uniqueness, objectivity, and understanding. Commercial design works are often highly recognizable, striking a balance between conveying information and expressing the art. As a result, the works created by illustrators with these abilities usually feature personalized expression techniques, contain flexible viewpoints and thinking, and visualize the conveyed information, so as to arouse the imagination of the audience.

But Mr. Sugisaki rarely uses illustration elements in his designs. How should one decide what visual elements are needed for a design project? Mr. Sugisaki believes that visual communication is holistic, and both text and illustration are essentially types of visual expression. In the design conception stage, the divergence of key words and key images, that is, the combination of language elements (words) and visual elements (points, lines and planes) is his passionate way of expression. As the art director of the team, he will choose the appropriate way of expression based on the project's design concept through illustration, photography, copywriting, and others. He will also decide according to the production conditions and effects.

In the days before computers were popularized, Mr. Sugisaki completed each design by manually trimming the font spacing. It was only after his encounter with the first generation of computers in 1989 that he discovered that the essence of design is to combine visual information elements. As a result, he ventured into experimenting with arrangements and transformations between words and colors to obtain different visual effects and look for the fun of serendipity in them. To this day, Mr. Sugisaki speaks of design as if he were a newborn calf unafraid of the tiger and maintains his original aspirations. Mr. Sugisaki believes that necessary skills to be a designer include the ability to think and express oneself, a certain knowledge, and the ability to identify and solve problems.

1. ガラパゴス or Galapagosization, a Japanese commercial term, refers that an isolated area undergoes "self-adaptation" alone, thus losing the interchangeability with elements outside the area.

01

02

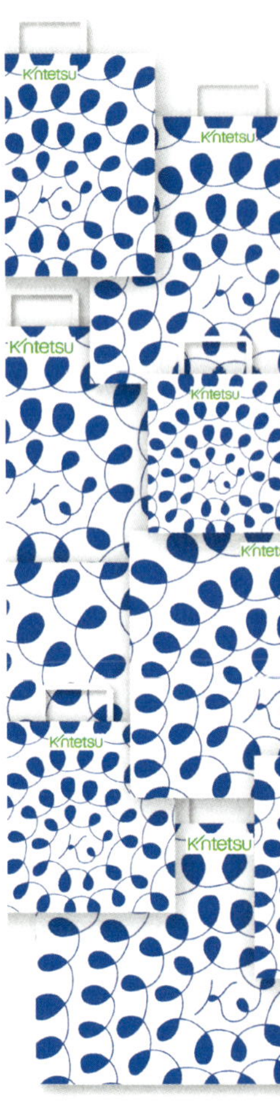

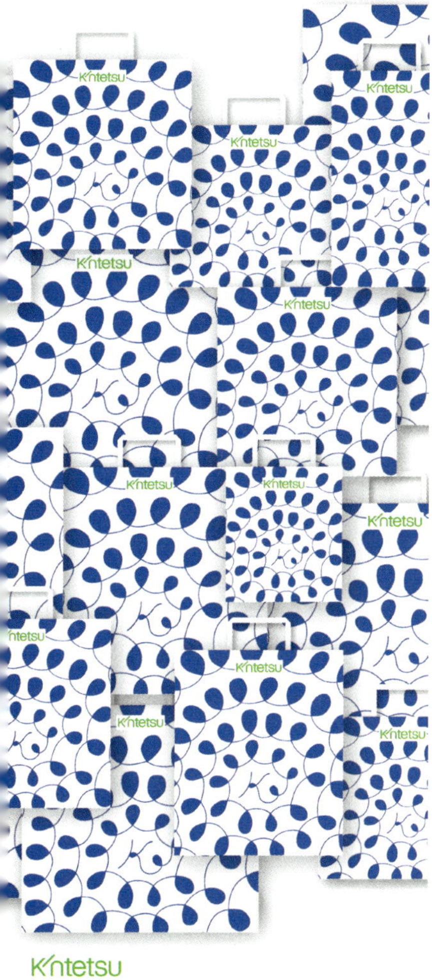

01. *Japanese Fan Exhibition*, 2006, Illustration: Ami Okamoto

02. *Shopping Bags and Wrapping Paper for Kintetsu Department Store*, 2013, Design: Yi Chin Wang

03. *Hangzhou Asian Games and Para Games Poster*, 2022

03

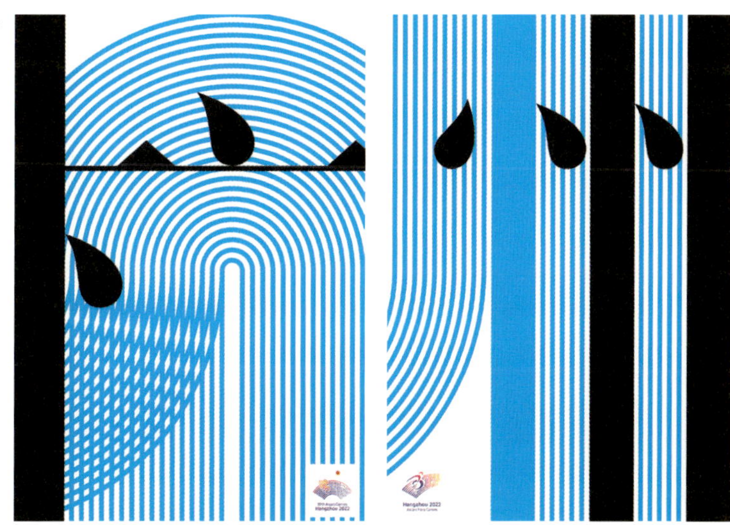

"The Japanese are perhaps better at discovering beauty in the smallest details or in inconspicuous changes."

Akiko Sekimoto

Akiko Sekimoto

Born in Tokyo in 1976, she got her Master's degree in Design from Tokyo University of the Arts in 2002. She established her personal studio Hidamari Ltd. in 2018 to use her expertise in graphic design to direct and develop for the renewal and launch of various brands, stores, and products. Her scope of work includes brand logo creation, product development, packaging design, store design, and others. Her classic designs are highly acclaimed and popular for years. She has won many awards including JAGDA New Designer Award, Japanese Package Design Awards, Red Dot Award, Hong Kong Global Design Award, Design for Asia Award, CS Design Award, Tokyo Art Directors Club Award, and others. She participated in the International Poster Triennial (IPT) in Toyama and the Festival international de l'affiche et du graphisme de Chaumont.

Akiko Sekimoto's contemplation resonates with the idea that "Japanese culture is a culture of observation." This culture involves observing nature, humans, animals, and plants, seeking the subtle and concealed "beauty" in the transient, the void, and the incomplete.

Japanese illustration industry is becoming increasingly diversified. What do you think about illustration with Japanese features?

I think there are some expressions that only the Japanese can present because many Japanese are dexterous and insightful. Although this trait is also often interpreted as weakness, I think it is this trait that gives these people their delicate and detailed expressive force.

Besides, Japan's highly variable seasonality allows us to appreciate the nuances. In addition, the Japanese are perhaps more adept at flat presentation like ukiyo-e and manga than the realistic and figurative expression.

Which Japanese illustrators' works have inspired you?

Tawaraya Sotatsu, Ogata Korin, Ogata Kenzan, and Hon'ami Koetsu.

When you choose an illustration as a visual element for a poster, what is the first thing you consider?

Whether it echoes my intention in creating the poster and whether I find enjoyment in it.
If the creator cannot feel happy from it, the work will not be able to move the audience.

What do you think are the differences between Japanese and Western aesthetics?

As far as beauty itself is concerned, I think it is the same. But the Japanese are perhaps better at discovering beauty in the smallest details or inconspicuous changes.

When illustrations are used in different scenarios, such as packaging, posters, and identity systems, do they give the work a stronger recognizability? Do you think there are design works that are not suitable to use an illustration?

In the case of illustrations used to express the main visual message, I think it is necessary to envision the scenario of use and think about the most appropriate way to present each part before arranging the layout.

In the case of an identity system, depending on the scenario of use, sometimes a figurative and expressive illustration may not be as effective as a "simplistic and plain" pictogram.

Do you think there is still a boundary between an illustrator and an artist? What do you think are the differences between the two?

Most of the time, the illustrator is working on the client's request, while the artist is expressing more of his own ideas. It is certain that there are a large number of people who do a job in these two aspects.

What features do you think an illustration that meets the needs of commercial design should present?

The ability to present the purpose of the production clearly and concisely. I think it is significant to communicate with the client during the production process and to enjoy the feeling of building the work together. In this way, you are not only completing the work, but creating a touching piece.

Q&A

D-BROS New Year Card

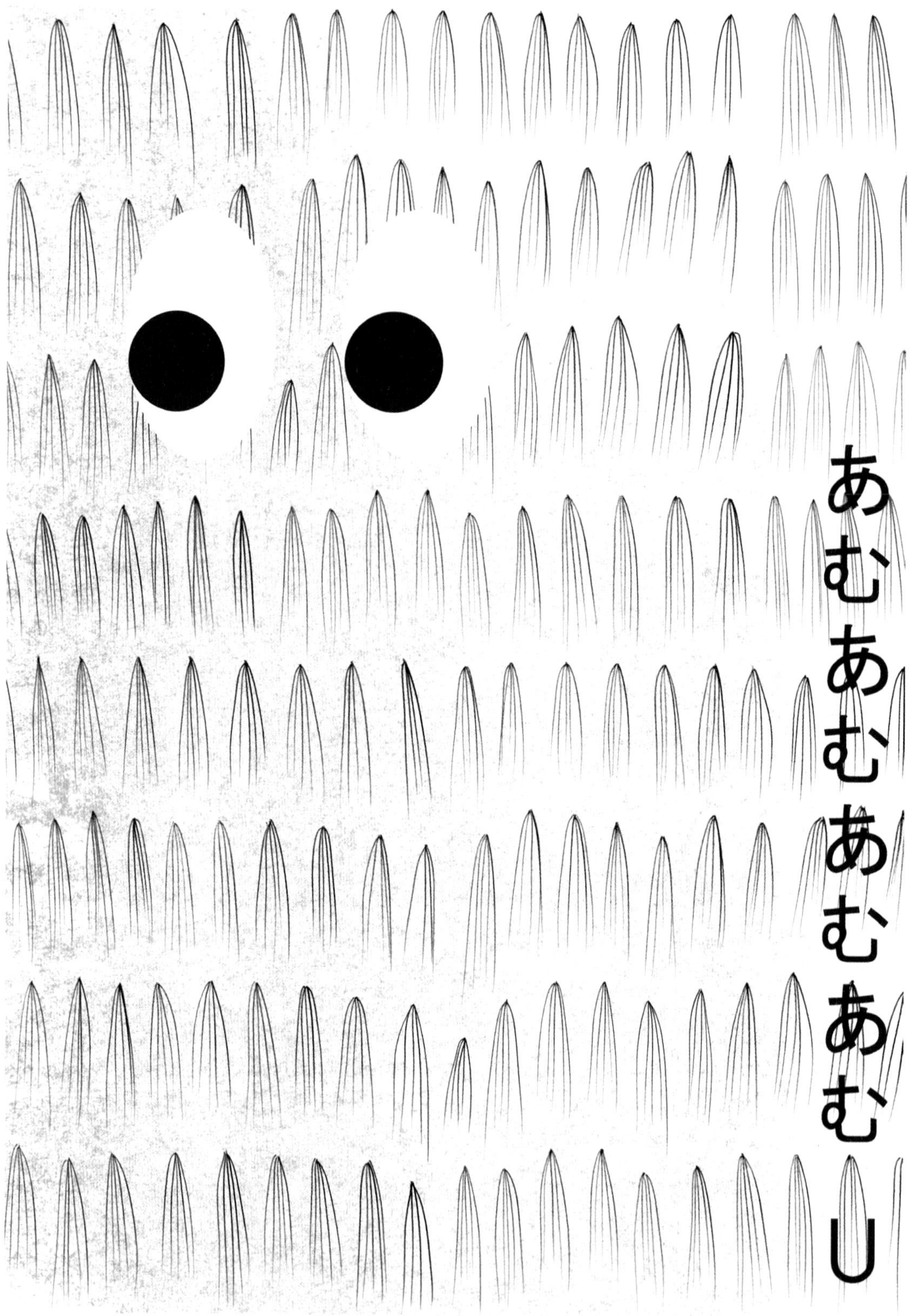
あむあむあむあむし

ちくちくちくちくし

Let's make it for U!

Let's make it for U!

U: Packaging and Visual Design for a Knitting Tool Recycling Store

"Illustration is an end in itself, and design is a means."

Hitoshi Akasako

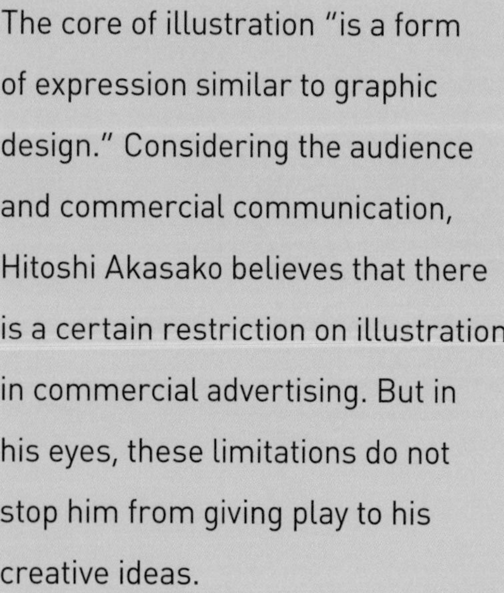

The core of illustration "is a form of expression similar to graphic design." Considering the audience and commercial communication, Hitoshi Akasako believes that there is a certain restriction on illustration in commercial advertising. But in his eyes, these limitations do not stop him from giving play to his creative ideas.

Hitoshi Akasako

He founded the creative studio THE END in 2013 and previously worked on various projects at Onuki Design Studio. He is responsible for all forms of art direction and communication-related design, including product development and advertising planning, in addition to design for television commercials, graphics, packaging, webpages, space, and others. He has been the winner of several awards including the ADC, TDC, and JAGDA, Japanese Package Design Awards, and others.

The Japanese illustration field is gradually becoming increasingly diverse. What do distinctive Japanese illustrations look like to you?

Japan is home to many distinctive illustrations, including contemporary works such as manga and anime, as well as traditional art. They all share a common charm: They feature simple, bare lines and silhouettes. Their core is a form of expression similar to graphic design.

Is there any work by seniors or illustrators in Japan that inspires you?

My designs are not influenced by any particular person or singular work. Instead, they may be deeply influenced by various subcultures. Skateboarding, for example, is one of them. I am often inspired by certain lifestyles, including related design, fashion, and music.

What do you think are the similarities and differences between the roles of an illustrator and a graphic designer?

Illustration is an end in itself, and design is a means. Designers use illustration to achieve a design effect and they need to consider the holistic visual presentation.

Could you please give an example of how you apply the essentials of illustration elements to your designs?

For example, when I design text visually, I mark shifting lines, shapes, and colors. It is highly similar to draw an illustration.

The elements of graphic design are always evolving. I have observed that the graphics in most of your works incorporate expressions or emotions. Is such an abstract concept more recognizable than the element of a concrete illustration?

They may look abstract because they retain only the most fundamental features to attract attention and leave deeper impressions on the audience. By using the minimum necessary elements, the illustration becomes a more powerful presence with a resemblance to a logo.

Your works give a sense of a visual balance. Which of the elements of illustration, graphics, text, and color combination would you consider using first in this balanced state?

The use of elements depends on the theme and intent of the whole work. It cannot be generalized.

Is there a restraint in the use of illustration in your work? Do you think there is a limitation or restriction to the illustrative element in commercial design?

Given the audience and intent, some limitations on illustration do exist in commercial advertising. However, these limitations will not affect giving play to creativity, so I have not felt too many difficulties.

Q&A

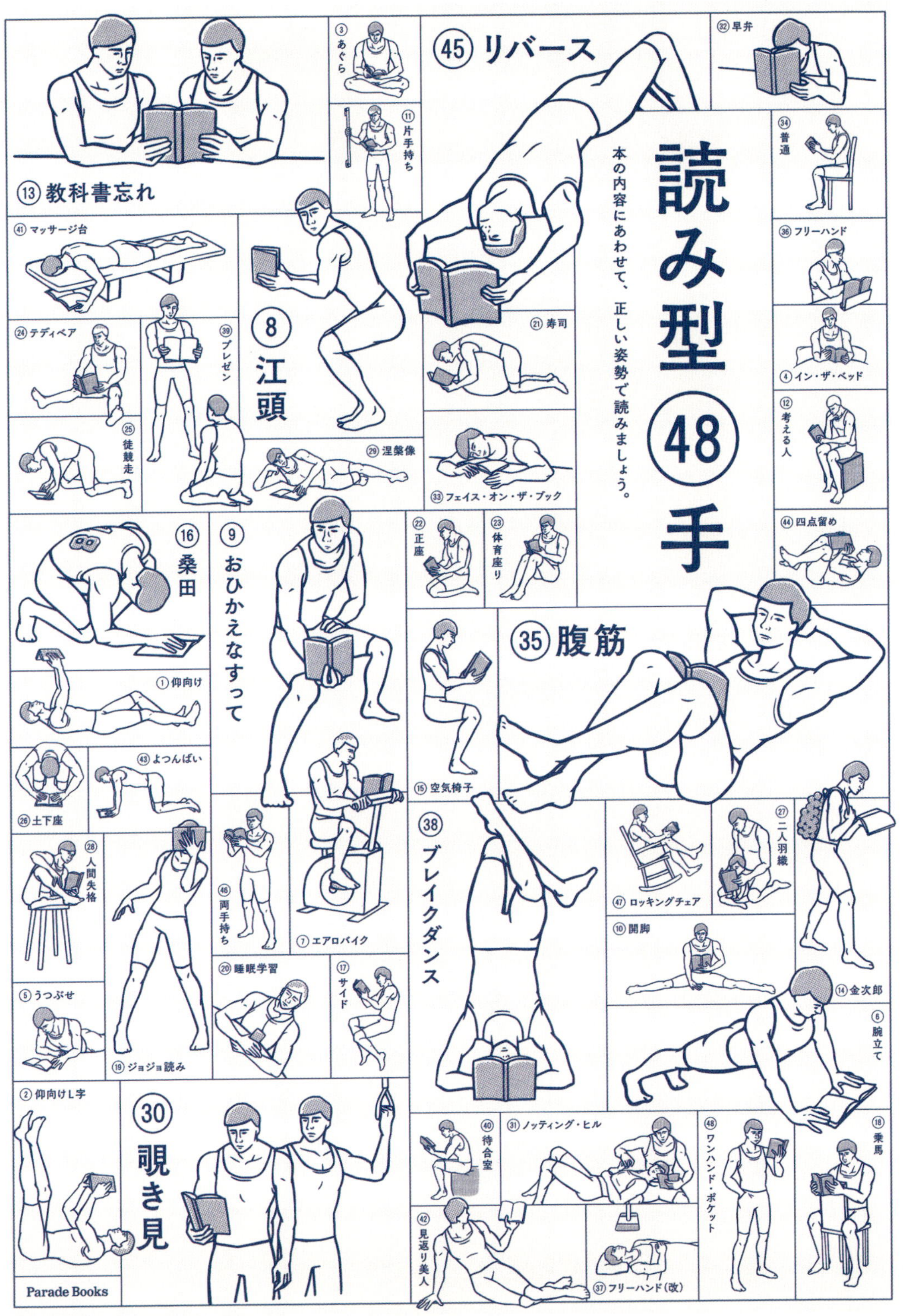

48 Reading Postures

"I build the image of the brand by the ensemble of photographic expressions, CG and illustrations."

Aoshi Kudo

"Ms. Hirano's monochrome series *Grey* had a great influence not only on me but also on the field of graphic design such as posters in Japan," said Mr. Kudo. He and Keiko Hirano, Designer and Visionary, founded Communication Design Laboratory to pursue modern functionality and aesthetics in design and to establish a unique style.

Aoshi Kudo

Aoshi Kudo is the President of Communication Design Laboratory (CDL). He graduated from Tokyo University of the Arts and joined Shiseido's Advertising Division in 1988. Mr.Kudo worked at Shiseido Paris for four years, starting in 1992. In 2005, he co-founded CDL with Ms.Keiko Hirano in 2005. Mr. Kudo's portfolio includes creative direction and designs for the beauty brands "IPSA" and "SHISEIDO PROFESSIONAL," as well as communication design and sign design for the Oita Prefectural Art Museum (OPAM).

He has received numerous awards, including the 2001 Mainichi Design Award, the New York Best Design Award from the American Institute of Architects, the iF Design Award, the ID-Award, the New York Festivals Awards Gold Prize, the Pentawards Gold Prize, the NY ADC Award Silver Prize, the Tokyo ADC Member Prize, and the Japan Package Design Awards Grand Prize. Mr.Kudo also serves as a part-time lecturer at the Department of Design at Tokyo University of the Arts.

Illustrations from different eras show different characteristics of the times. Could you please share which Japanese illustration works still have an important influence on you today?

A group of pastel illustrations depicting abstract forms by Keiko Hirano in the 1980s still has a major influence on me today. We might debate whether or not they can be classified as illustrations, but since they were heavily used in commercial media such as books and record jackets, let us consider them as illustrations. In the latter half of the 1980s, an illustration style called "Heta-uma (bad-good)" was mainstream in Japan, but Ms.Hirano's works suddenly expressed a completely different new world from that of the Heta-uma or realistic style which had existed earlier. I feel that the monochrome series called "Gray," which Ms. Hirano developed later, (though they might be more difficult to be thought of as illustrations) had a great influence not only on me but also on graphic designs such as posters in Japan.
Other creators whom I consider epochs are Yoshio Hayakawa, Eijin Suzuki, Pater Sato, and Noriyuki Tanaka.

Q&A

There is an increasing number of diverse illustration drawing styles emerging in Japan, what kind of impression do you think Japanese illustration has left on you in recent years?

Many of the illustrations today are used mainly for descriptive purposes, or I feel that they are used as decorative backgrounds that do not express a sense of individuality.

What do you think has changed in the application of Japanese illustration today compared to the past? Could you please give an example of how illustration in everyday life gives you pleasure?

Until the 1990s, illustrators possessed their unique creative characteristics, and their illustrations were made to come alive in places where they belonged. Nowadays, it seems that projects are generated after illustrators present what they think are versatile expressions. As a result, the characteristic illustrations no longer exist, and we witness many illustrations that share a similar broad direction with slightly different personalities that are easy-to-use. (I'm sure there are unique illustrations, but they don't appear in places that many people can see.)

Do you think there is still a boundary between being an illustrator and artist? What do you think are the differences between the two?

I think this is not a difference in the style or expression of the painting, but a difference in the way of life.

I think that an illustrator cannot be an artist, but an artist can be both. I think it's not about what's better, but how an individual wants to live. That is an individual's free choice.

I have observed that you rarely use illustration elements in your projects. In your opinion, how should one select the visual elements needed for a project?

The orientation of visual elements is determined by the inevitability or suitability of the project. It's true that there aren't many package designs that use illustrations in recent years, but I still use illustrations a lot in my branding projects. Please refer to https://www.ipsa.co.jp/.

I build the image of the brand by the ensemble of photographic expressions, CG and illustrations.

What features do you think an illustration that meets the needs of commercial design should present?

I think that an illustrator should have a unique creative style that only he/she/they can express, as well as the ability to respond to (clients') requests while making the most of the style.

SHISEIDO PROFESSIONAL SUBLIMIC
Creative Director/ Designer: Aoshi Kudo
Coloring Director: Keiko Hirano
Client: SHISEIDO PROFESSIONAL

IPSA THE TIME RESET AQUA LIMITED
Creative Director/ Art Director/ Designer: Aoshi Kudo
Logotype Designer: Helmut Schmid
Client: IPSA

"A sense of quality that emerges from an exquisite universe."

Yasuhiro Sawada

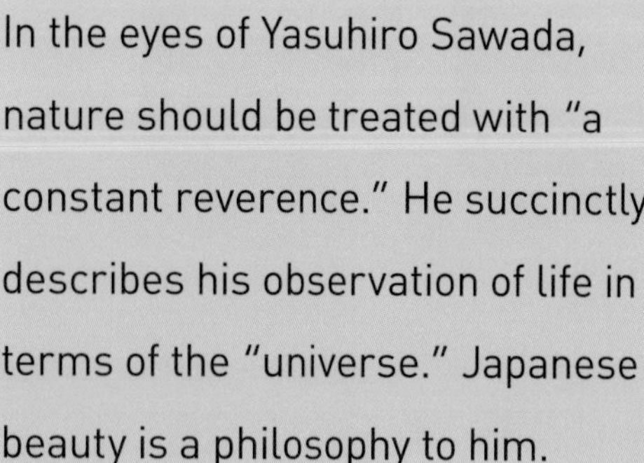

In the eyes of Yasuhiro Sawada, nature should be treated with "a constant reverence." He succinctly describes his observation of life in terms of the "universe." Japanese beauty is a philosophy to him.

Yasuhiro Sawada

He was born in Tokyo in 1961. He graduated from the Department of Design, Tokyo University of the Arts in 1986. After working at Suntory till 1989, he established the Yasuhiro Sawada Design Studio. In 1991, he held his solo exhibition "P2" at Graphic Gallery in Ginza. His awards include New York ADC Silver Prize 1988, Bronze Award at the IPT in Toyama 1988, Grand Prize at ADC Tokyo in 1989, Gold Award at Japan Magazine Advertising in 1990, Tokyo ADC Award in 1990, JAGDA New Designer Award in 1993, and others. He is a member of Tokyo TDC and JAGDA, the Alliance Graphique Internationale (AGI), and Professor at Tama Art University.

Please give an example of what kind of spirit Japanese aesthetics represents in your eyes.	Treat nature with great constant reverence.
What do you think are the differences between Japanese aesthetics and Western aesthetics?	The difference lies in how they interpret and treat realism.
Which Japanese drawings or illustrations have ever touched you? How have these works inspired you in your design career?	I am proud of the unique Japanese expression way of "Rinpa."
Have you ever appreciated or admired any Japanese artists? What enlightenment have they brought to you in your pursuit of aesthetics?	A lot, and I got a great deal of benefit from them.
Could you please share with us the projects you have been working on recently? Through what do you incorporate your observations of life into your designs?	The exquisite universe.
Your works span product, space, exhibition, and graphic design. What do you think are their common points? Your graphic design works are highly distinctive. Does this distinctiveness have anything to do with the design principles you promote?	A sense of quality that emerges from an exquisite universe.

Q&A

Graphic Design of Yasuhiro Sawada

"Contemporary illustration has always provided us with new values and ways of looking at things."

Kazuo Kuribayashi

Since design connects all elements related to human beings, such as society and nature, Kazuo Kuribayashi believes that the everyday world, which is changing all the time, can be seen in contemporary illustration, and that new ways of thinking and new joys can be acquired from them.

Kazuo Kuribayashi

He graduated from Tama Art University in 1988 with a degree in Graphic Design. After working for TSTJ Inc., he founded kuri+ graphic in 2001. He held the "KAZUO KURIBAYASHI POSTER EXHIBITION / 2009—2019" in Hangzhou, China in 2019. He obtained the TDC Award in 2013. He is a member of Tokyo TDC and JAGDA, and lecturer at Joshibi University of Art and Design.

Q&A

Could you please share with us the impact of Japanese illustration on you through an unforgettable experience?

Every time I interact with other designers and their works, I feel like I come across new values, and my brain seems to become more active. All these give me unprecedented pleasure.

Are you influenced by other Japanese artists and how do they inspire you in your creation?

For about a decade from 1990, I worked under Yukimasa Okumura. That period taught me how to breed new values like never before.

Do you think there is still a difference between illustrators and artists in drawing art today, when the boundaries are getting increasingly blurred? Also, what do you think are the genes of Japanese art that can be found in contemporary Japanese illustration?

I think certain boundaries are indeed vanishing. For example, in *Cracked Ice*, Maruyama Okyo uses a few strokes to "leave blank space" in the center of the painting. In this way, although the painting itself is flat, it presents a sense of depth that is different from that of the perspective representation. This marks one of the features of Japanese art.
There are many other similar features. I think modern Japanese graphic design has successfully inherited them.

What do you think contemporary Japanese illustration has brought to the world? How does it differ from Western or Chinese drawing?

Contemporary illustration has always provided us with new values and ways of looking at things. Regarding the difference between Japanese illustration and Western and Chinese drawing art, as I mentioned before, "It lies in leaving blank space."

It's not difficult to see that you combine elements of imagery and drawing in your work. Please take "*Light More*" as an example and tell us about the message you want to convey.

I grew up with such a feeling that, in my eyes, all living things have seemed to be "surrounded by a warm light." Although no one has deliberately taught me this, I have always felt a light around me whenever I felt happiness, since I was five when I was torn between life and death and eventually recovered from my illness.

This work leverages typography to express the joy I felt when I was able to hold a solo exhibition in Hangzhou, China.

Every creation is a self-reflecting journey. Were there any surprises in creating the "*Inujima Life Garden*" series? What is the core of this series?

This work is the VI (Visual Identity) of the "*Inujima Life Garden*". The so-called notion of VI is the graphic expression of a certain team's philosophy. This time, the main elements used are "earth," "air" and "light." Inujima, an island made of rocks, is located in Okayama Prefecture. With the poorly drained soil and excessive light throughout the year, it is not really suitable for the natural growth of plants. But even so, the plants on that island are still growing freely and beautifully with the help of human power. I chose to leverage the eyes of the staff of the botanical garden to recreate the images of inujima's natural environment and the staff dedicated to the study of plant habitats.

You are still striving to observe life and find beauty in it. In your opinion, what is the sense of beauty of Japanese people?

I think it lies in the switch of perspective. When you look at things from a different perspective, you may find a whole different side. The Japanese sense of aesthetics lies in this discovery and presentation of beauty from the spots unnoticed by others. But this sense is perhaps originally inherited from China since ancient times.

Despite the passage of time, you seem to have maintained an optimistic and bright mind and kept creating. What kind of fields do you plan to try in your future artistic journey?

If people are given a sense of happiness when they meet my work, then I want to build a "space." It need not be my "personal art museum," but a more personal "café" where we can get to know each other better. Besides, I hope that it is also a warm field surrounded by light.

Inujima Life Garden

Light More

"Illustration has no boundary."

Takafumi Kusagaya

Illustration is an artistic language that is both a bold and autonomous expression of the individual and an objective and honest expression of society.

As a designer, Takafumi Kusagaya conveys to the audience that the value of design is "for the happiness and daily life of human beings."

Takafumi Kusagaya

He was born in 1963 in Shizuoka Prefecture. He graduated from his major in literature in Tamagawa University. In 1996, he opened a design company called "Kusagaya Design" to deal with graphic design, including posters, advertisements, and flyers. He held solo exhibitions at HB Gallery, Omotesando, Tokyo in 2016, and Takeo Store, Aoyama (Tokyo) in 2019. From 2016 to 2017, he was invited to participate in the MADE IN JAPAN exhibition in France as a representative of Japanese graphic design. From 2017 to 2019, he served as a communication design consultant in DNP. He was awarded the JAGDA New Designer Award in 1995, the Good Design Award in 2001, the Nikkei Advertising Award in 2005, the Asahi Advertising Award in 2008, the Asahi Advertising Award (Grand Prix), and others. He is a member of JAGDA and Tokyo TDC.

From the Showa Period to modern times, there are many classic Japanese illustrations and animation works that have grown up together with generations. Do you have a particular favorite illustrated character?

In Japan, the boundaries between class and occupation are greatly blurred. The manga I read as a child, including those by Fujio Akatsuka, Fujiko Fujio, illustrator Makoto Wada, and genre-less artist Tadanori Yokoo, are quite enjoyable for me. On the contrary, I do not like some anime works with more rigid world views.

Contemporary illustration is becoming increasingly diverse. What do you think are the features and charm of Japanese illustration?

As I mentioned before, illustration has no boundary. Compared to other countries — for better or worse — Japanese illustration has a weaker sense of differences, and because of this, it is able to have a bolder and more autonomous expressive force.

How did you learn the art of illustration and drawing? Is there any way to improve one's painting skills?

I am completely self-taught. As opposed to painting with immersion in myself, I seem to be better suited to creating promotional materials like the sort of theatrical posters with a purpose in a team. It allows me to express myself more objectively. Meanwhile, I was able to be more open to receiving and interpreting people's feedback on my work.

In your work, illustration is an artistic language with a unique expressive force. What do you think are the differences between drawing and illustration?

I don't know what you mean by drawing here. However, if drawing is a "private work" then illustration is a "work objectively presented to society." If these two creations can be in complete agreement, is it not a kind of joy from the supremacy of the expressive force?

The illustrations in your work *Direct Marketing Report 2017* (産直レポート 2017) are highly vivid and interesting. How did you come up with this idea?

The orders from clients are often highly commercial in nature, but I want to use them to express the "utopia" in the minds of everyone who lives in the present. At the same time, this work is also my tribute to Virginia Lee Burton, whose book *The Story of Life*[2] has arguably shaped my outlook on life.

On social networking sites, you also seem to be devoted to studying illustration. Is this a kind of study? Could you please elaborate on that?

I am more interested in who created what works than in telling what I have done and how I feel about creating it. I want to present the process of creating the work as much as possible through the standpoint of the creator, and from there, to communicate with others.

Q&A

2.The book *The Story of Life* tells about the history of the Earth from its origin to the present.

Bobby Womack (2016)

Track (2013)

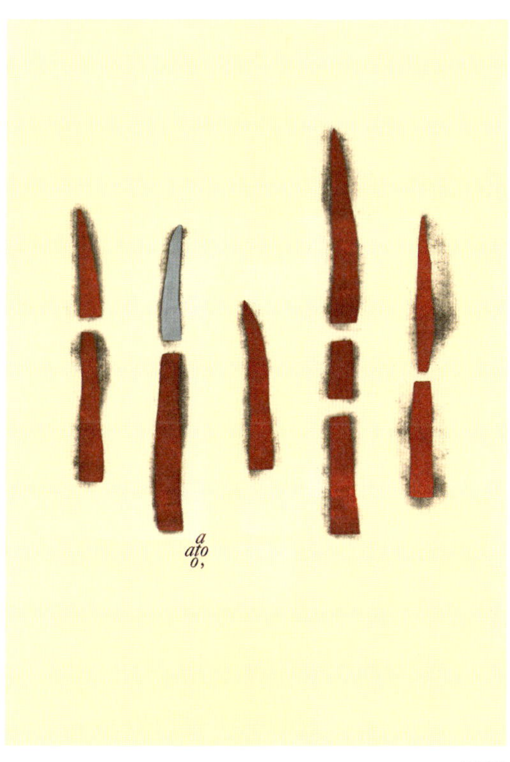

ato (2000)

Unite (2012)

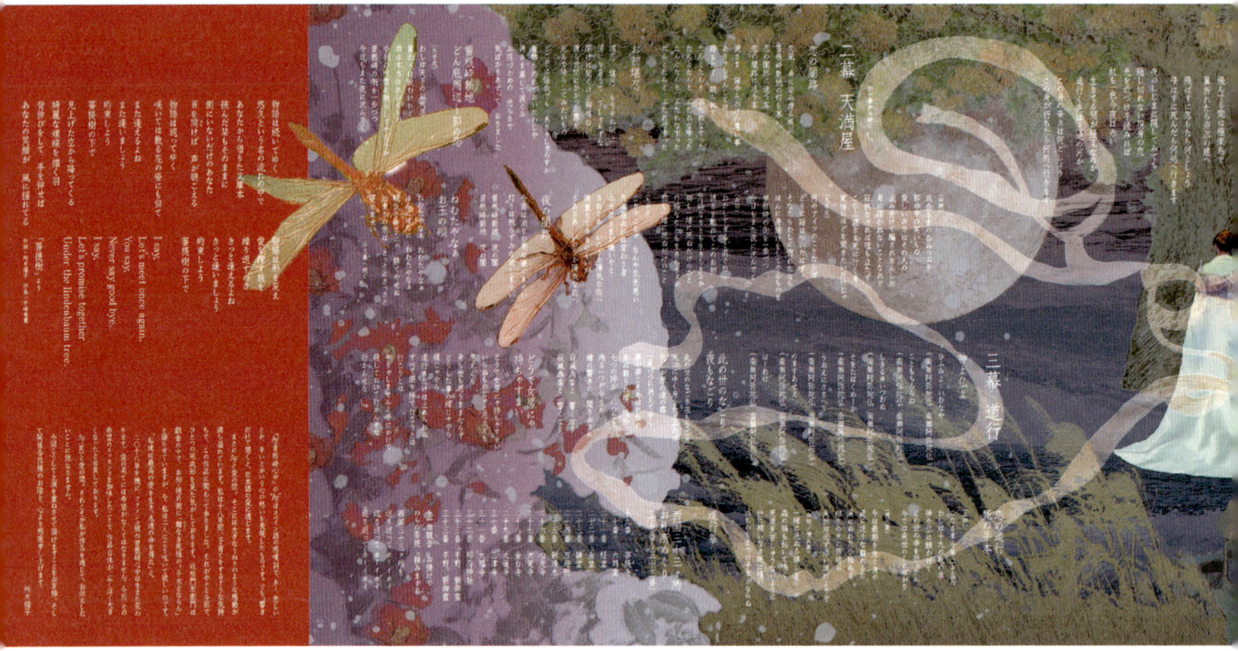

二幕　天満屋
三幕　道行
I say,
Let's meet once again.
You say,
Never say good bye.
I say,
Let's promise together
Under the lindenbaum tree.

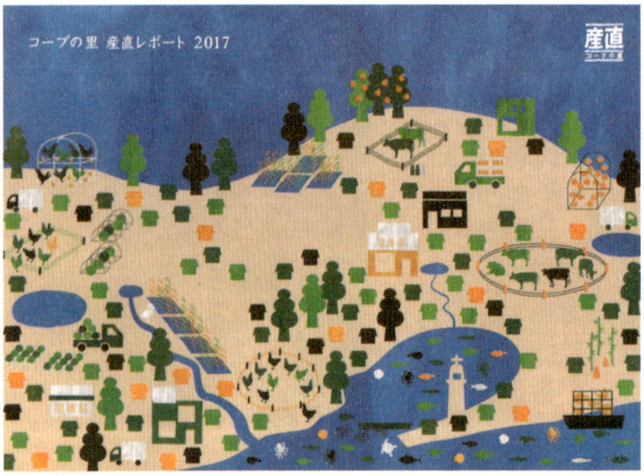

コープの里 産直レポート 2017
産直
コープの里

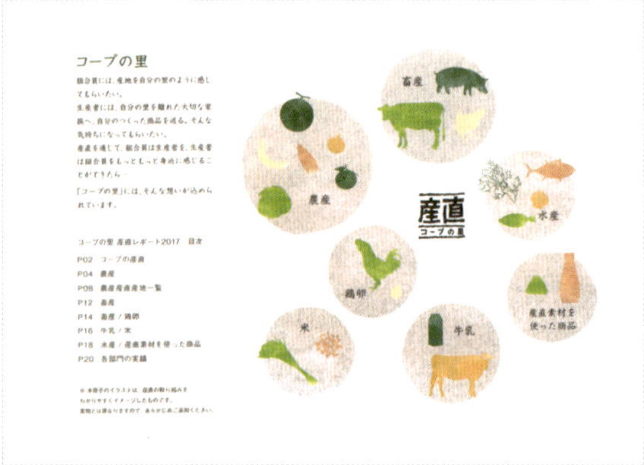

コープの里
組合員には、産地を自分の里のように感じてもらいたい。
生産者には、自分の里を離れた大切な家族へ、自分のつくった商品を送る。そんな気持ちになってもらいたい。
産直を通して、組合員は生産者を、生産者は組合員をもっともっと身近に感じることができたら…
「コープの里」には、そんな想いが込められています。
コープの里 産直レポート2017　目次
P02　コープの産直
P04　農産
P08　農産産直産地一覧
P12　畜産
P14　畜産 / 鶏卵
P16　牛乳 / 米
P18　水産 / 産直素材を使った商品
P20　各部門の実績
畜産
水産
農産
産直
コープの里
鶏卵
米
牛乳
産直素材を使った商品

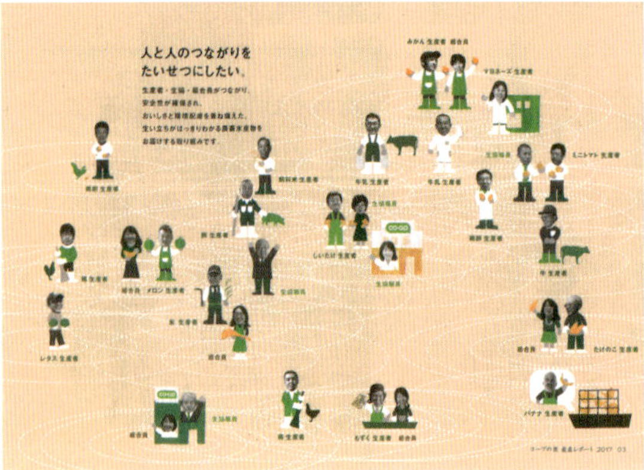

人と人のつながりを
たいせつにしたい。

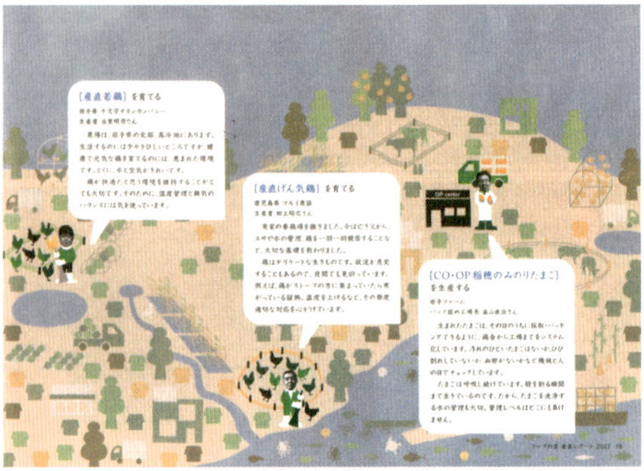

[産直若鶏]を育てる
[産直げん気鶏]を育てる
[CO・OP稲穂のみのりたまご]を生産する

Ay曽根崎心中

地獄のように
美しく
極楽のように
恐ろしい

Ay Sonezaki Shinju (2018)

Direct Marketing Report 2017

H.B

"The diversity of illustration is what makes them so charming."

Muramatsu Takehiko

The charm of Japanese illustration is its "diversity." According to Muramatsu Takehiko, along with the changing times and human lifestyles, the development of Japanese illustration and graphic design will give birth to new values and a new aesthetic consciousness.

Muramatsu Takehiko

He was born in Fuchu city, Tokyo in 1983. He graduated from Tama Art University in 2006 with a degree in Graphic Design. After working for an advertising production company, he started his own business in 2010. Before 2016, he was also the assistant of Koichi Sato. He is in charge of the website "Graphic Designer's Local Customs and Stories in Tokyo." He is a member of JAGDA and Tokyo TDC and a graphic designer of MU DESIGN ROOM.

Contemporary Japanese illustration is highly diverse. Who do you think best represent the Japanese features in the past illustrators?

Katsushika Hokusai. In Japan, recreational activities for the common people developed mainly during the Edo period. It was thanks to the near absence of warfare at that time (the rise of modern Japanese subculture is also inseparable from the development of recreational activities during this period). Ukiyo-e is one of the representatives. Hokusai can be said to be the pinnacle of "the general public as the main," "the subject matter of all things" and "the method of reproduction." He can also be said to be the source of the development of the later unusual manga.

When did you first get involved in illustration? What do you think is the charm of Japanese illustration at the moment?

I am a graphic designer myself, and as a result, there may not be a clear time node to formally get in touch with illustration. If I must tell the time, I think it was my third year in university when I made a poster in class.

The diversity of illustration is what makes them so charming. Along with the development of manga and anime, the illustration art has continued to break new ground. In Japan, pure art has not developed to the extent of a subculture, which has enabled illustrators to flourish in this "blank space."

When you choose an illustration as a visual element for a poster, what do you consider in advance?

Most of my illustrations are applied to exhibitions and personal works, and as a result, most of them are drawn by myself in the form of private designs. Specifically, it may focus on the following aspects: the presentation between drawing and text, the expression between design and illustration, and the emotions or wildness assigned to the vector data often use forms of expression that are considered "indigenous" and "rustic" in the medium of communication with Asian countries.

Q&A

You used to be Koichi Sato's design assistant. What was your daily work like at that time? How has this experience influenced your design?

I worked as his assistant at the time when his business was downsizing and overall work was easier.

He enjoyed his work very much. But after the posters are completed, he would start discussing how to better improve the work. He was happy in it but never satisfied. He always has a persistent and endless pursuit of beauty.

In the past, illustration and graphic design were not yet completely "divided as two fields." Koichi Sato was among the last creators of that era and the first designer after the two "had been divided as two fields." I aspire to be a designer like him.

I'm afraid I would be ceaseless if I were to go on and on about Mr. Sato's story. It will probably seem to be exaggerating. But I'm also trying to forget about him now (in an attempt to have fewer constraints on future creation).

When illustrations are used in different scenarios, such as packaging, posters, and identity systems, do they give the work a stronger recognizability? Do you think there are design works that are not suitable to use an illustration?

Sometimes there are specific circumstances where I feel a pictogram would be more appropriate for the expression. But I really haven't thought much about the specific differences between illustration and pictogram.

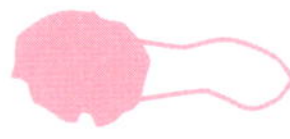

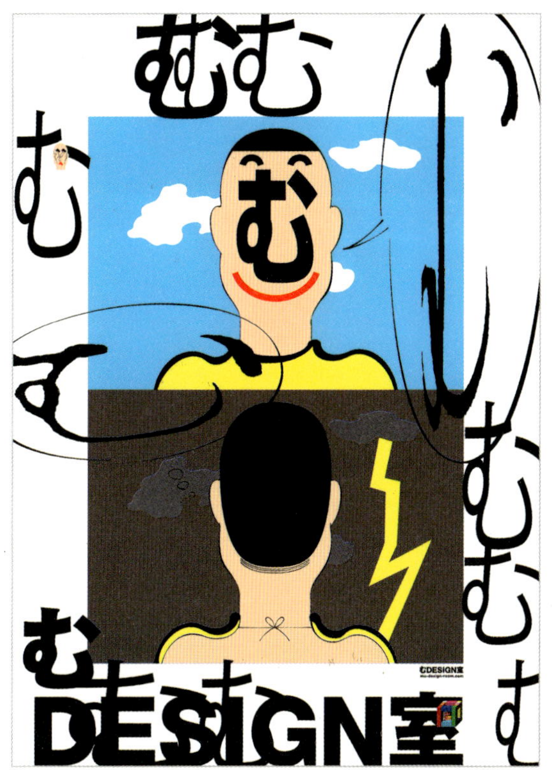

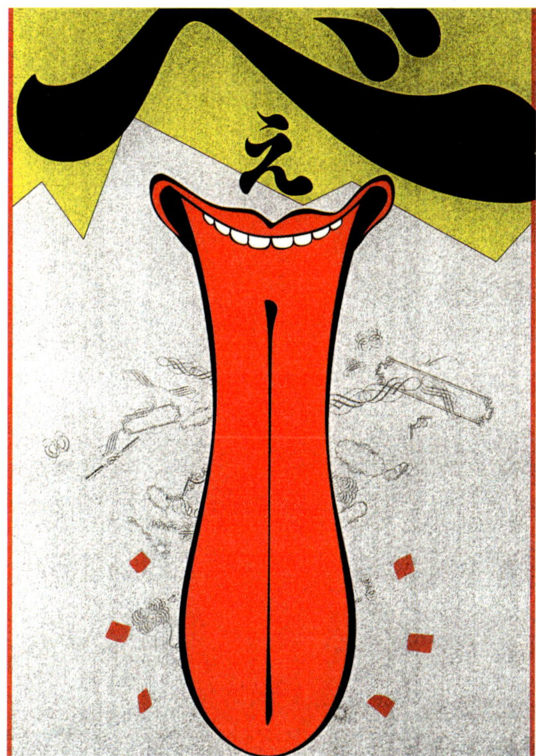

Series of works themed in Japanese

Series of works themed in Japanese

む
むDESIGN室

むDESIGN室
DESIGN

む
(め)

の

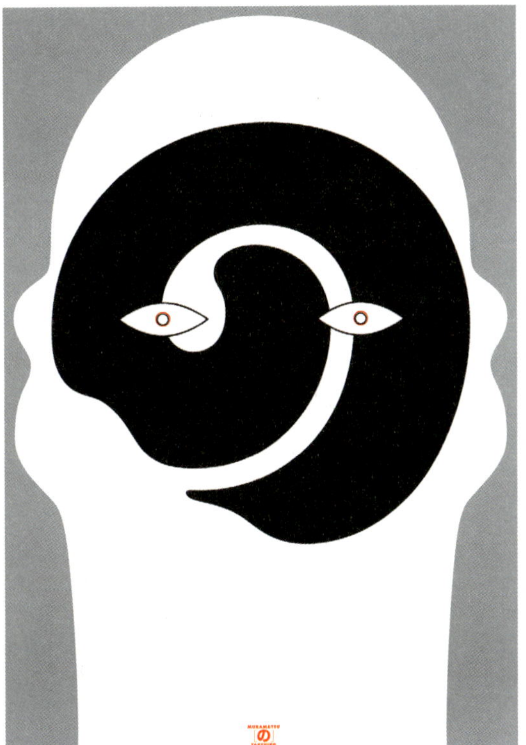

Series of works themed in Japanese

LET'S EAT!
HAVE A NICE DAY

Osamu Harada

SEEING DREAMS IN ILLUSTRATION

Chapter

"You can start choosing your direction now for whatever field you want to have in your future as an illustrator. Thinking about what you are passionate about and what you are good at doing will make your journey easier. Keep your curiosity about the world and share your resonance through illustrations that can be shared with many people."

Osamu Harada

Osamu Harada was one of the most important Japanese illustrators who established the Japanese Kawaii trend. He graduated from Tama Art University with a degree in graphic design. He has achieved professional success through his interest and passion for drawing. He has created a series of classic IP images and driven the success of his personal brand OSAMU GOODS.

Poster of "Osamu Harada: Finding Kawaii" Exhibition in Setagaya Literary Museum

Leaflet of "Osamu Harada: Finding Kawaii"
Exhibition in Setagaya Literary Museum

Mother Goose
Mother Goose
Mother Goose
Address Diary Little Book Book
KEY
PLAYING CARDS
Laundry
ERASER
OSAMU'S MOTHER GOOSE
OSAMU'S MOTHER GOOSE
Swimming Season
OSAMU GOODS
OSAMU GOODS

Roy
ROGERS
Come On RANGERS!
THE SINGING COWBOY
ワッペン

EXHIBITION

45th Anniversary
1976-2021

12 April - 22 May 2022 PALETTE CLUB

Poster of "OSAMU GOODS 45th Anniversary"
Exhibition in Palette Club

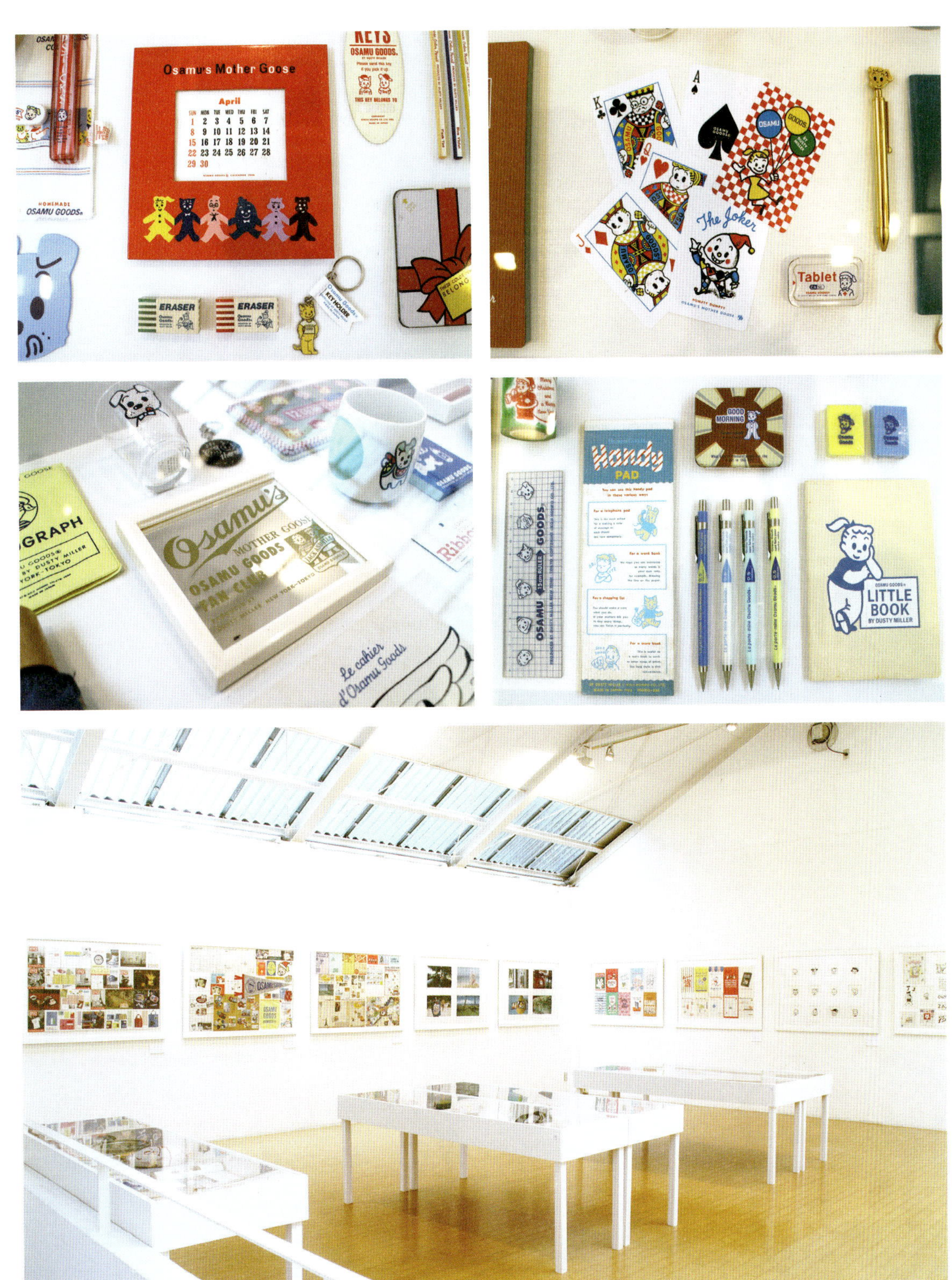

Photograph: design studio paperweight INC.

ジル
JILL

ジャック
JACK

ベティ
BETTY

ハンプティ・ダンプティ
HUMPTY DUMPTY

オールドマザーグース
OLD MOTHER GOOSE

リトルピッグ
LITTLE PIG

ドッグ
DOG

キャット
CAT

カウ
COW

ジョージー・ポージー
GEORGIE PORGIE

ダンス トゥ ユア ダディ
DANCE TO YOUR DADDY

アイ シー ザ ムーン
I SEE THE MOON

Born in Tokyo, Japan in 1946, Osamu Harada developed a keen interest in drawing from an early age. At the age of seven, He began studying under the Japanese abstract artist Minoru Kawabata. Osamu Harada was born in the year following the end of World War II. During this period, Japanese people were influenced by American culture to a greater or lesser extent, and Osamu Harada was no exception. His parents ran an imported food store. Among the piles of American canned goods in the store were Campbell's soup cans that Andy Warhol had "turned into gold." The cans' label design and bright colors have sowed the seed of design in Osamu Harada's heart.

In addition to being heavily influenced by American culture, the artistic atmosphere of Japanese society at that time was one of the key scenes in Osamu Harada's early aesthetic education. Meanwhile, living in Tokyo, Osamu Harada is uniquely positioned to expose himself to traditional Japanese culture. Traditional performing arts such as Kabuki and Rakugo, as well as new plays, have become sources for him to absorb Japanese culture.

While receiving his education in Aoyama Gakuin Senior High School, Osamu Harada visited Shibuya, Ginza, Akasaka, and other places to supplement his knowledge beyond books. At that time, there was a grocery store called American Pharmacy in Hibiya, specializing in American daily groceries, newspapers, magazines, and others. For Osamu Harada as a teenager, the grocery store was a small world full of the exotic atmosphere that he longed for. The moment he stepped into the store, it's like walking through the Dokodemo Door into the United States. This is also the reference sample for Osamu Harada to establish Osamu Goods. After graduating from high school,

Osamu Harada entered Tama Art University to study graphic design. During this time, Osamu Harada attended an illustration course taught by Japanese designer Yuzo Yamashita. In 1969, Osamu Harada completed his college course. Immediately after graduation, he went to the United States to study illustration techniques, where he was greatly influenced by the Pop Art and related manga techniques of the time.

Before he formed a set of artistic outlook and knowledge system that could be fully leveraged, Osamu Harada was like an indefinitely expandable canvas, absorbing the culture of domestic and foreign pioneers or classical traditions, allowing the two colors to mingle and splash on the canvas, and letting the lines and blocks of color under his brush carry his emotions.

After a year of study in the United States, Osamu Harada returned to Japan in 1970. In the same year, he designed the cover of the inaugural issue of *an·an*, a well-known Japanese magazine. At the age of 24, Osamu Harada officially launched his career as an illustrator. By chance, He received the admiration and encouragement of Seiichi Horiuchi, who was the art director of *an·an* magazine at the time. Osamu Harada subsequently created a series of cover illustrations for *POPEYE*, *BRUTUS*, and other magazines under the direction of Seiichi Horiuchi. He was also responsible for the covers of magazines such as *Bikkuri House* and *Roman Fantastique*. According to Osamu Harada's statement in his book *Osamu Goods Style*, in the early days, to become an all-around illustrator, he had studied about 10 drawing styles in five years to meet the needs of different types of illustrations.

In addition to the publishing industry, Osamu Harada was also involved in creating projects for the advertising industry. In 1976, Osamu Harada created the mascot "Potato-boy" for the Calbee potato chip series, and this classic character has been used till today, more than 40 years later. In addition, he also created the mascot for Hitachi's "White Bear" air conditioner series in 1980. Osamu Harada turned his passion for drawing into a profession, drawing one classic cover illustration and brand mascot after another. The motive power gained from his interest became the core of Osamu Harada's further expansion of his career.

In 1976, at the suggestion of Shizuo Ishii of Koji Honpo, Osamu Harada decided to transform his characters into products and established the brand OSAMU GOODS. OSAMU GOODS has been popular among Japanese high school students due to the cute and diverse characters and the practicality of the products. The brand has established the unshakable position of Osamu Harada in the Japanese Kawaii trend.

The success of the brand is inseparable from two decisions made by Osamu Harada: brand positioning and design choices.

"There is nothing more devoid of design value than an item that has no use," said Osamu Harada. This triple negative argument can be said to be the main theme of OSAMU GOODS' brand positioning. Through OSAMU GOODS, Osamu Harada embedded his illustrations into people's daily lives. Tote bags, lunch boxes, handkerchiefs, cups, stationery... Most of the illustrated product he chose are rooted in daily necessities, which, whether presented in combination with design or illustration, are acceptable to consumers.

In this way, Osamu Harada bestowed a layer of art to daily necessities. According to Osamu Harada, "For illustration to be loved by people, it is necessary to use elements that are universal, understandable, and shared by anyone as the main body of the illustration."

In addition, Osamu Harada had a different perspective on product design.

In his view, one cannot create a good product without excellent design abilities. Even if the illustration elements used are the same, the different choices in terms of product, production process, and presentation reflect the designer's personality. Osamu Harada possessed both perspectives as an artist and a designer. The products created by him are the result of his balancing and integrating these two perspectives.

Although branded IP images have only started to become a hot topic of discussion in recent years, Osamu Harada had already achieved commercial success 46 years ago through a series of character roles created by him. In the eyes of Osamu Harada, an illustrator is not considered an artist, but an entertainer who delights the viewer. He maintained that the fun part of illustration is its entertaining nature. He created illustrations to see people's happy facial expressions. As a result, he was also good at depicting some light-hearted and bright works. Commonly seen are images of little boy Jack, little girl Jill and Betty, egg man Humpty Dumpty, kittens, puppies, or others on OSAMU GOODS' products. The creation of these characters is inspired by the famous *Mother Goose*, a British collection of nursery rhymes in which one can find the names and songs corresponding to the characters.

Close observations easily reveal the ingenuity of Osamu Harada's characterization. In these 12 classic characters, boys and girls, old men and babies, humans and animals, and smiling and crying faces all coexist. Osamu Harada did not shy away from condensing his observations of life into these characters.

These classic character images indicate that Osamu Harada's style was formed under the combined influence of American comics, pop art, and the Showa Period in Japan at the time.

The skillful lines, the use of contrast colors, the bright and eye-catching color choices, and the handling and presentation of textures are the elements that characterize this series of characters.

In addition, the public can also speculate when the illustration was created by Osamu Harada by the change in the way the eyes are drawn. From the early days of his creation to the early 1980s, Osamu Harada was deeply influenced by American comics techniques. During this period, the eyes of his characters usually showed a small triangular notch, which is the eye shape commonly seen in American comics. With the passage of time, Osamu Harada gradually found that this shape limited him from creating characters other than children, so he ventured away from the fixed form and replaced the eyes with an oval shape. At present, the small triangle in the eye is like an easter egg hidden in the illustration by Osamu Harada, which makes it more interesting to admire his works; it feels like a treasure hunt.

In addition to developing his career and brand, Osamu Harada cared deeply about the development of the interests of the next generation and their growth and education. He has passed on traditional Japanese knowledge and drawing techniques to the next generation by drawing illustrations, establishing an illustration academy, teaching in person, and other forms.

In 1997, Osamu Harada rebuilt his former home next to Tsukiji Market in Tokyo and established the illustration academy Palette Club School, which brought together literary and artistic figures such as illustrators, publishers' editors, and picture book writers to serve as teachers and openly recruited students interested in illustration and picture books every year, with the purpose to impart professional illustration knowledge to the younger generation. After Osamu Harada passed away in 2016, Palette Club School remains on its mission to inspire and educate, continuing to provide systematic classes for illustration enthusiasts. It has Jun Iida, Kazuyoshi Iino, Kiyoshi Kuroda, Jin Kitamura, Atsuki Kikuchi, and

Kazunari Hattori as course lecturers, actively supporting those with interests and dreams.

Osamu Harada once shared a quote with students, saying: "You can start choosing your direction now for whatever field you want to have in your future as an illustrator. Thinking about what you are passionate about and what you are good at doing will make your journey easier. Keep your curiosity about the world and share your resonance through illustrations that can be shared with many people."

Originally published in *BranD* Magazine, Issue 63, edited by Gakky Luk, translated by Pan Yingzhao

Reference: *OSAMU' s A to Z*, written by Osamu Harada. Akishobo, 2019

OSAMU'S A to Z

原田治の仕事

AKISHOBO

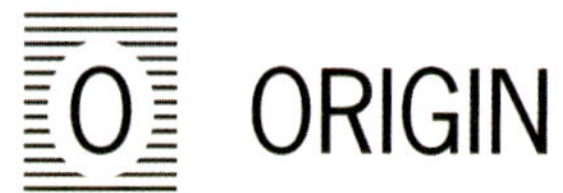

スケッチブック 1955年 (9才)

絵が得意だった原田は7歳の時から抽象画家、川端実のアトリエに通い始めた。幼少時のスケッチや絵日記が数多く残されている。著書『ぼくの美術帖』の鈴木信太郎の項では、10歳前後に、祖母の養生に同行して通っていた箱根の温泉旅館にあった鈴木信太郎の絵を真似てパステルで画帳に描いた思い出を綴っている。

雑誌表紙 「ビックリハウス」1975年7月号/1976年9月号/1977年1月号、8月号/1978年2月号/1979年6月号、9月号/1980年4月号、10月号 PARCO出版

C COVER

雑誌表紙 「ビックリハウス」1980年7月号 PARCO出版

「POPEYE」1980年7月25日号 平凡出版

HAPPY
BIRTHDAY
TO YOU
OSAMU
HARADA

HAPPY
BIRTHDAY!

HA
HA
HA
HA
HA

HA
HAPPY
BIRTHDAY!
OSAMU
HARADA

ペン 1992年

キーホルダー 1991年 s

1981年

1995年 s

パスケース 1991年

1995年 s

ポーチ／ペンケース 1983年

1995年 s

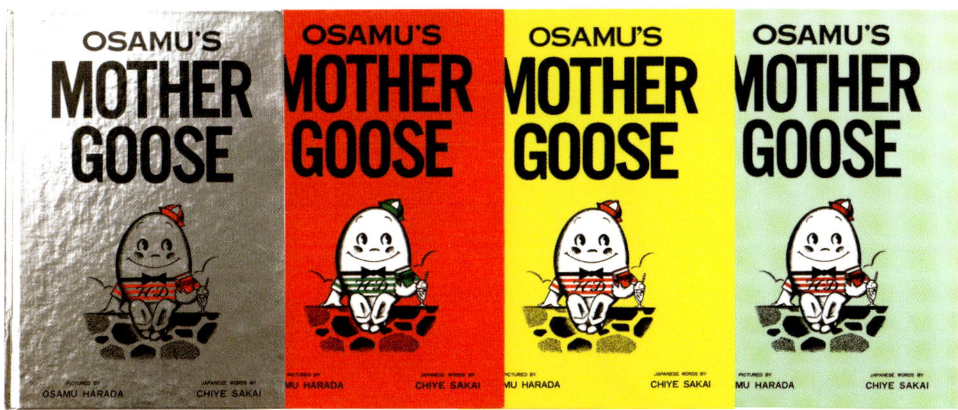

1刷（銀）1976年、2刷（赤）1984年 コージー本舗／復刻版（黄）2001年 勁文社／復刻版（緑）2018年 復刊ドットコム

布製絵本 1976年

OSAMU GOODS®
COMPANY
from the "Mother Goose"
English fairy tales
BY
OSAMU HARADA

THIS LITTLE PIG
This little pig went to market;
This little pig stayed at home;
This little pig had roast beef;
And this little pig had none;
And this little pig cried,
"Wee, wee, wee!"
All the way home.

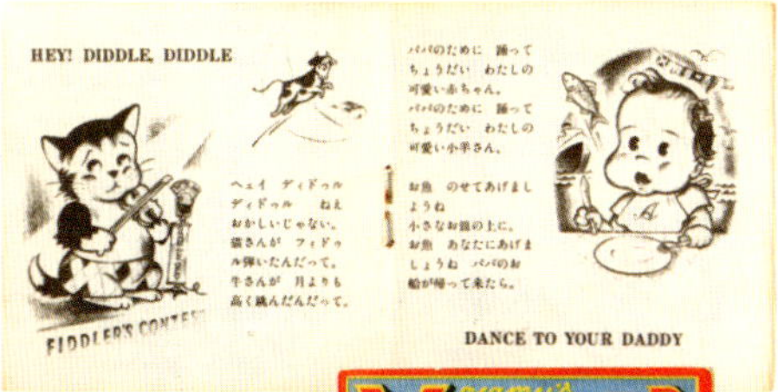

HEY! DIDDLE, DIDDLE
ヘェイ ディドゥル
ディドゥル ねえ
おかしいじゃない。
猫さんが フィドゥル弾いたんだって。
牛さんが 月よりも
高く跳んだんだって。
FIDDLER'S CONTEST

パパのために 踊って
ちょうだい わたしの
可愛い赤ちゃん。
パパのために 踊って
ちょうだい わたしの
可愛い小羊さん。

お魚 のせてあげましょうね
小さなお皿の上に。
お魚 あなたにあげましょうね パパのお
船が帰って来たら。
DANCE TO YOUR DADDY

osamu's
MOTHER GOOSE
YOUR FIRST
LITTLE BOOK

ノベルティ 1970年代後半

1970年8月5日号

1971年11月5日号

1971年11月20日号

1972年2月20日号

空すべて C90
BL30
C90+Y70
イラスト(版下 0.1mmのスミ線)はすべてあたりケイです
白ヌキ
髪・まゆ・目・DはBL100
外側のケイ線(版下別に有り)はすべてY100+M100 けぬき合せ
Y100+M100
肌色Y40+M40
鼻・Y100+M100
Y100+M100
C100+M50
C70+M70+Y20
海・C70+Y50
C90+Y70
白ヌキ
髪・まゆ・目・DはBL100
Y40+M40
Y100+M100
空すべてY70
BL30
白ヌキ
C100+M50
白ヌキ
空・白ヌキ
BL=100
C90+Y70
BL30
BL=100
C70+M70+Y20
海・C70+Y50
C90+Y70
Y40+M40
Y40+M40
白ヌキ
白ヌキ
空Y70+M60
Y70
Y70
BL=100
白ヌキ
C70+M70+Y20
Y100+M100
Y40+M40
海の色・C100+M50
BL=100
Y70+M60

Originally published in OSAMU`s A to Z, Akishobo, 2019

Works

CONTEMPORARY ERA IN ILLUSTRATION

Chapter

現代美術への入り口としての伝統文化。

Traditional Culture Is The Portal to Contemporary Arts.

伝統

滑板武士
挑戰和勇敢的靈魂
捲土重来
獅子奮迅
對極限運動
熱情已經印在了滑
的基因中，正是這種動
使我們每天進行創新
一直在努力為我們的
帶來最佳的運動世
@danilokato

Cover Design for Vinyl *MOTHRA*

This is the illustrator's cover and interior for the *MOTHRA* vinyl soundtrack set, featuring a 12-inch poster of the twin girls and Mothra. Mothra, a giant moth-like creature symbolizing motherhood in Toho's monster movie series, is depicted with bold, vivid colors and dense brushwork, creating a visually powerful impact.

Illustrator: Yuko Shimizu **Project Client:** Waxwork Records

Tips:

The symmetrical Mothra creates a balanced composition, with the twin girls integrated as its mirrored sides. The vibrant colors of the large screen give the illustration an overall exotic feel, while the red sun behind represents Japanese characteristics.

C0 M74 Y98 K0
C13 M36 Y95 K0
C3 M3 Y84 K0
C63 M76 Y53 K53
C62 M33 Y8 K0
C92 M68 Y35 K19

HUEY

Nihonga Series

This collection blends traditional Japanese style with modern actions, resulting in captivating digital illustrations inspired by Japanese paintings.

Illustrator: Danilo Kato

Project Clients: Melissa, Paramount+, MTV, Globo, SESC

Tips:

The illustrator blends "past" and "present" worlds, expressing reverence for the past and hope for the present and future. The technique of blurring time enables a constant shuttle between the two. Delicate lines and a traditional color palette add vibrancy to the visuals.

C3 M73 Y69 K0
C20 M90 Y100 K0
C25 M100 Y95 K25
C1 M7 Y17 K0
C4 M48 Y64 K0
C11 M37 Y76 K0
C58 M38 Y69 K13
C65 M46 Y66 K27
C79 M67 Y22 K5

はっこうや

発酵食

HOLIDAYS

手洗い

マスクをする

距離を保つ

HAKKOYA

発酵食

HAKKOYA

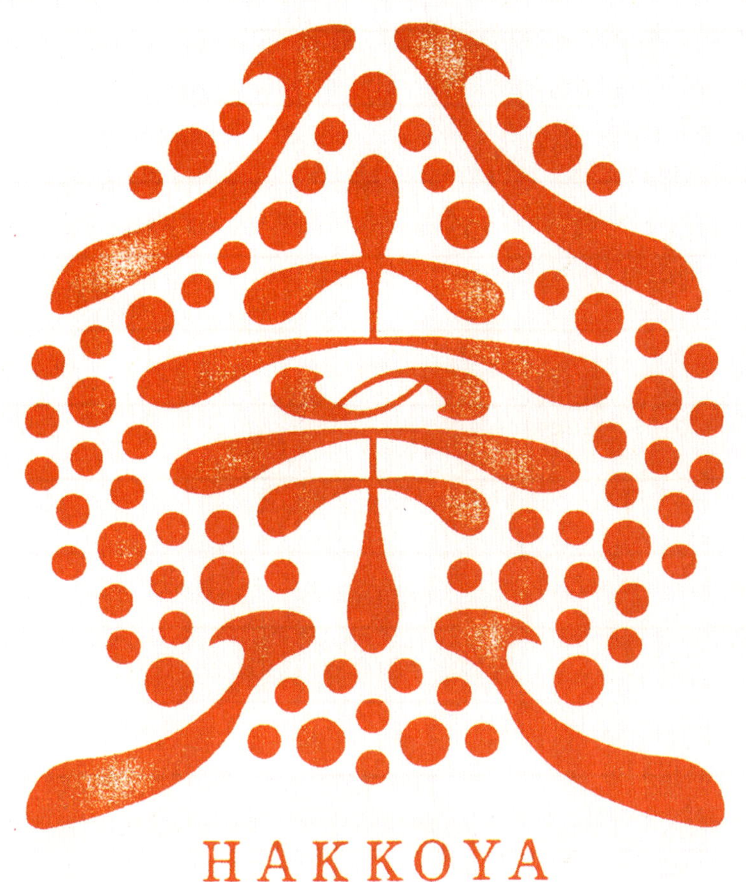

HAKKOYA

HAKKOYA in Nagoya, Japan, sells pickles, sake kasu cheese, sake kasu fish, miso-marinated pork, and more. Popular holiday posters rotate in-store. A Covid-19 prevention poster emphasizes handwashing, mask-wearing, and fermented foods.

Illustrator: Hidekazu Hirai
Design Studio: Peace Graphics
Project Client: Yamatoya Moriguchizuke Souhonke Co.,Ltd

Tips:

Posters' illustrations align with the main visual " 幸 " character and the brushstrokes, unifying the brand's visual identity and leaving a lasting impression.

- C0 M90 Y100 K0
- C0 M0 Y0 K5
- C0 M0 Y0 K100

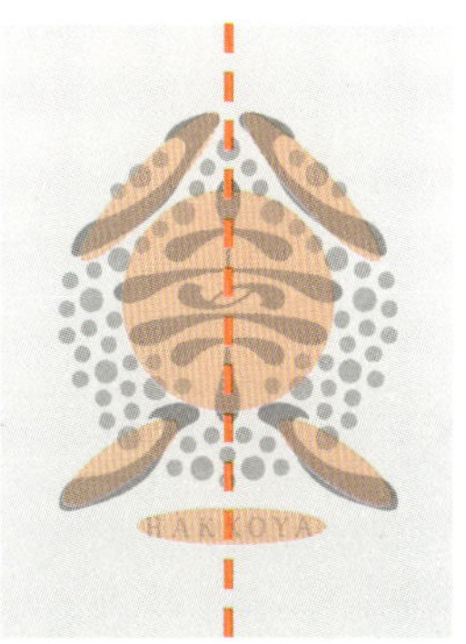

新井勉
非器の城
五代将軍徳川綱吉、
登場する。
これより世に不幸を撒き散らす。
批評社
書き下ろし本格時代小説

Cover for *Hikinoshiro*

The cover impressively depicts the Shogun (the title of the military dictators of Japan during the ancient times), leaving a lasting impression. The proud figure holds a traditional Japanese building, reinforcing their extraordinary stature in people's minds.

Illustrator: Kyonosuke Takayasu **Book Designer:** Shintaro Usui
Project Client: Hihyo-Sha publishing Inc.

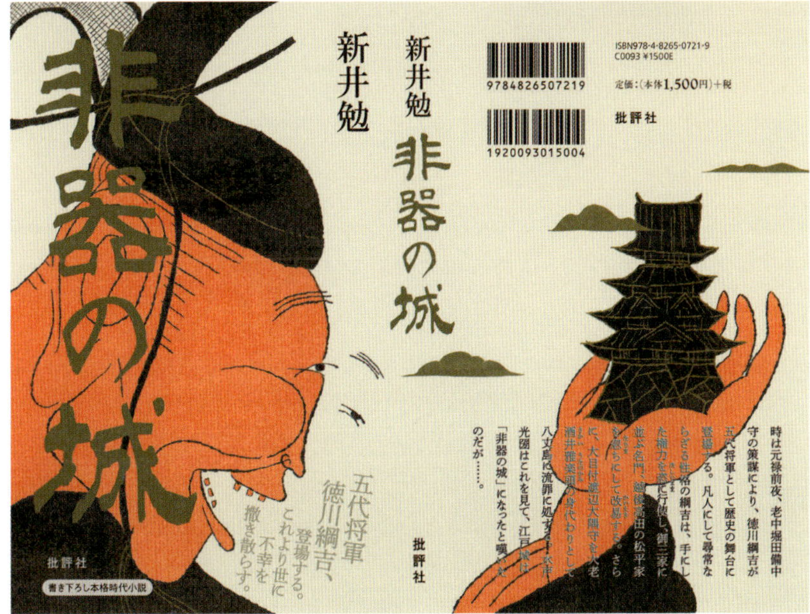

Tips:

Taken place in Japan's Edo period, the story inspired the illustrator to choose a Japanese lacquer painting style and a yellow-red color palette. Character illustrations prominently stand out in the artwork.

- C11 M79 Y84 K0
- C15 M13 Y22 K0
- C64 M58 Y82 K16
- C75 M73 Y74 K44

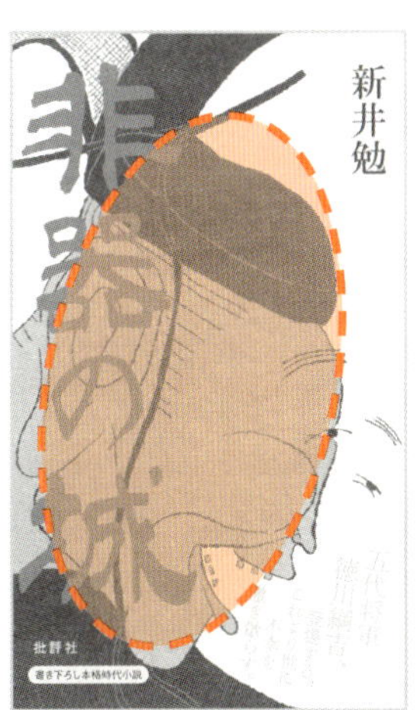

名古屋
六行亭
Nagoya Rokugyoutei
コーチン
手羽先
Nagoya Cochin Chicken wings
Miso taste
味噌味

名古屋
六行亭
Nagoya Rokugyoutei
コーチン
手羽先
Nagoya Cochin Chicken wings
Soy sauce taste
醤油味

名古屋
六行亭
Nagoya Rokugyoutei
国産赤鶏
手羽先
Japanese Akadori Chicken wings
Miso taste
味噌味

名古屋
六行亭
Nagoya Rokugyoutei
国産赤鶏
手羽先
Japanese Akadori Chicken wings
Spicy taste
ピリ辛味

Package of "Rokugyotei Tebasakini" Chicken Wings

This product is a soy sauce-seasoned chicken wing made from Nagoya Cochin, a premium breed of chicken. Traditionally sold as train station souvenirs, the gold packaging represents Nagoya Cochin, while the silver represents native Japanese red chickens. The limited production inspired the designers to convey gratitude through the packaging.

Illustrator: Fumiaki Muto
Art director: Hidekazu Hirai
Design Studio: Peace Graphics
Project Client: Yamatoya Moriguchizuke Souhonke Co. Ltd.

Tips:

The illustrator used ukiyo-e style to depict Japanese chicken breeds. The golden background represents "Nagoya," the city of the Tokugawa Shogunate. Vibrant red hues contrast with the background, creating an eye-catching effect for the chickens' portrayal.

C20 M73 Y70 K0	C36 M38 Y79 K0	C86 M80 Y71 K56
C30 M91 Y89 K0	C50 M52 Y91 K2	C69 M61 Y58 K9
C70 M82 Y67 K39	C80 M52 Y75 K13	C63 M78 Y43 K3

Wakayama "Ninomiya" Wagashi Store's Cockfighting Bun Packaging

This packaging design is for a specialty product from Ninomiya wagashi store, near the Tokei-jinja Shrine in Tanabe City, Wakayama Prefecture. The shrine is known as the "Cockfighting Shrine" due to the legend of cockfighting during the Battle of Dan-noura in *The Tale of the Heike*. The leader of the Kumano pirates held a cockfight between a red and white rooster to determine which side to support. The red represented the Taira clan, and the white represented the Minamoto clan. Ultimately, the White Rooster emerged victorious, leading the Kumano pirates to join forces with the Minamoto clan. The lid of the box is designed for playing "paper sumo."

Designer: Keiko Oogami

Photography: Shinichiro Uchida Photocreative

Tips:

Hand-drawn brushstrokes enhance the ancient, traditional feel inspired by the legend, adding historical and cultural appeal to the packaging.

- C46 M0 Y2 K0
- C0 M0 Y70 K0
- C0 M88 Y80 K0

南紀田辺

令和
REIWA

FUKUWARAI

A sake barrel design for a celebration in Marunouchi, Tokyo, marking the new name of an era, Reiwa. Fukuwarai is a popular Japanese New Year's game where blindfolded players try to place features on face drawings in the correct positions.

Design Studio: GOO CHOKI PAR

Tips:

The designer combines shapes, colors, and lines to create composite "faces," blending tradition and modernity with a playful and experimental approach.

- C49 M96 Y99 K27
- C25 M39 Y90 K0
- C61 M89 Y82 K50
- C90 M61 Y75 K29
- C0 M0 Y0 K100
- C99 M95 Y55 K8

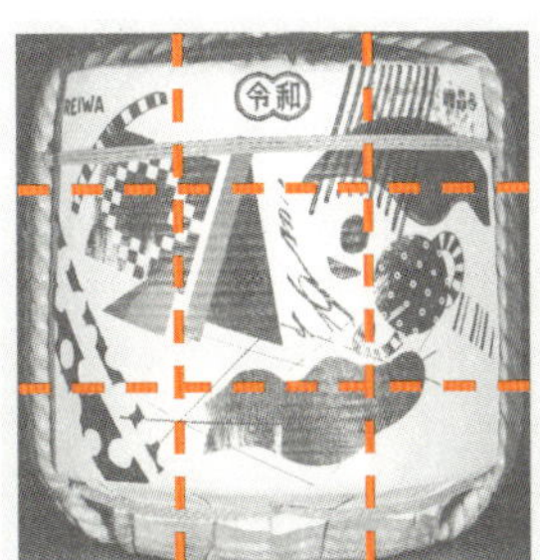

Tips:

The designer uses hot stamping to enhance the artwork's visual appeal. Traditional colors combined with modern elements create a strong design and visual contrast.

C44 M76 Y72 K5

C23 M48 Y73 K0

C100 M100 Y56 K13

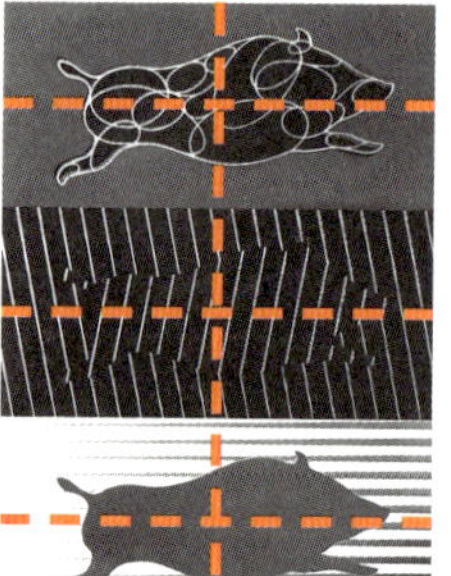

New Year's Card & Poster 2019

This is a New Year greeting card design for 2019. It was the Year of the Pig in the Chinese zodiac. The symbolism of this zodiac sign is to go straight ahead regardless of the situation and to charge forward with great ardency. This illustration depicts a wild boar filled with energy, which keeps moving forward in all weathers.

Designer: Ayaka Shimizu

Kifujin to Karajishi

This is a digital artwork inspired by the French tapestry series "La Dame à la Licorne," with Chinese and Japanese artistic styles. It is also a fan art that integrates Eastern and Western art styles, expressing the designer's tribute to the "Japanese-Western eclecticism."

Illustrator: Danilo Kato **Clients:** Melissa, Paramount+, MTV, Globo, SESC

Tips: The left and right symmetrical layout of the composition, the fusion of the Eastern and Western artistic elements make the whole painting harmonious and delicate.

C29 M80 Y85 K26
C36 M78 Y84 K42
C51 M65 Y73 K54
C27 M25 Y37 K0
C32 M33 Y89 K3
C22 M61 Y85 K8
C71 M54 Y49 K25
C62 M56 Y44 K18
C75 M69 Y56 K57

お好み焼
みっちゃん
井畝満夫の店
総本店

昭和二十五年創業。
広島の復興とともに、生まれ育った味。

お好み焼
みっちゃん
井畝満夫の店
総本店

昭和二十五年創業。
広島の復興とともに、生まれ育った味。

MICCHAN Advertising Visual Design

This is a series of advertising visual design proposals provided by the designer for MICCHAN company. MICCHAN is the first company in Japan specializing in Okonomiyaki, the soul food of Hiroshima, Japan.

Design Studio: IC4DESIGN

Tips:

The illustrator depicts the scenery of Hiroshima from a wide-angle perspective, capturing intriguing and captivating details when zoomed in. The sepia-toned color palette creates a nostalgic and traditional Japanese atmosphere.

- C10 M94 Y90 K0
- C0 M40 Y89 K0
- C0 M18 Y40 K0
- C62 M64 Y65 K8
- C55 M36 Y66 K0
- C12 M0 Y0 K0

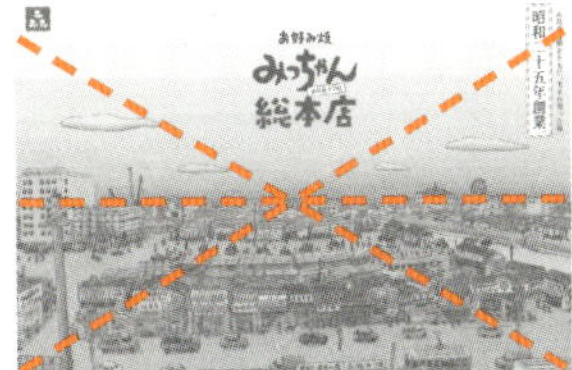

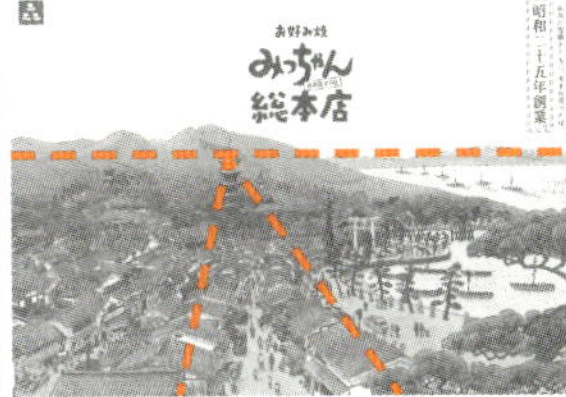

瀬戸内レモン
LEMON FACTORY
SETOUCHI LEMON
エスト エットのジュレ

瀬戸内フルーツ
est-etto

瀬戸内レモン
LEMON FACTORY
SETOUCHI LEMON

瀬戸内フルーツジュレ

瀬戸内フルーツジュレ ネーブルの島

瀬戸内フルーツジュレ レモンの島

瀬戸内フルーツジュレ 夏柑の島

❶

Works by IC4DESIGN

❶ *Setouchi Fruit Gelée*: The illustration is from the "Setouchi Fruit Gelée" (Setouchi jelly) series of Aohata's new brand "est-etto." The illustrators were inspired by Setouchi's marine landscape.

Design Studio: IC4DESIGN **Clients:** est-etto (Aohata Corp.), NHK

❷ *NHK YAMAGUCHI*: This is an illustrated poster created by the illustrator for NHK (Japan Broadcasting Corporation), showcasing the customs and traditions of the entire Yamaguchi City. To make this artwork visually appealing and engaging, the illustrators preserved the spatial relationships of various characteristic locations such as temples and foot baths, aiming to help the viewers better understand and promote Yamaguchi City. The rich content captivates attention, while the hometown connection adds a nostalgic touch.

Tips:

The composition ranges from foreground to background, offering a panoramic view with intricate details that pique viewers' curiosity.

- C6 M100 Y100 K0
- C0 M59 Y99 K0
- C82 M30 Y100 K19
- C55 M26 Y0 K0
- C92 M79 Y0 K0

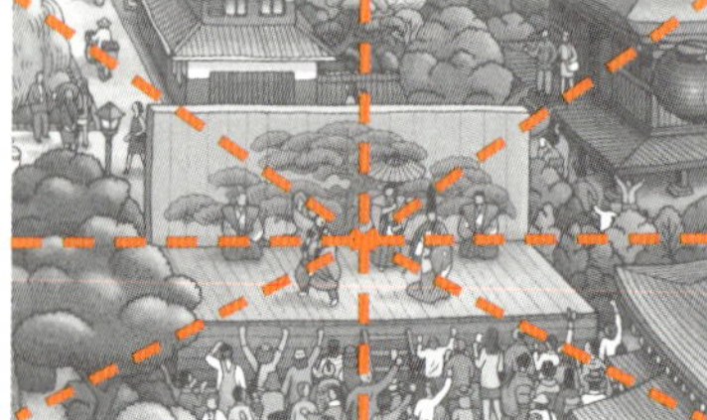

❷

Rio Spring Festival

This artwork was created using woodblock printing techniques and further enhanced through digital processing to achieve the desired visual effects.

Illustrator: Yukihira Nagao

Client: CLUB RIO

Tips:

The artwork features a symmetrical layout and combines traditional woodblock printing with digital processing for visual effects. The blend of print texture and digital typography enhances the artwork's aesthetics and glamour.

C3 M61 Y19 K0

C2 M38 Y99 K0

C64 M2 Y47 K0

C38 M31 Y31 K60

C65 M34 Y0 K0

C87 M35 Y47 K1

春の訪れを一緒に探そう
リオの春まつり
2019.3.24(sun)
10:30-16:00(少雨決行)
www.club-rio.link

for girls
for girls

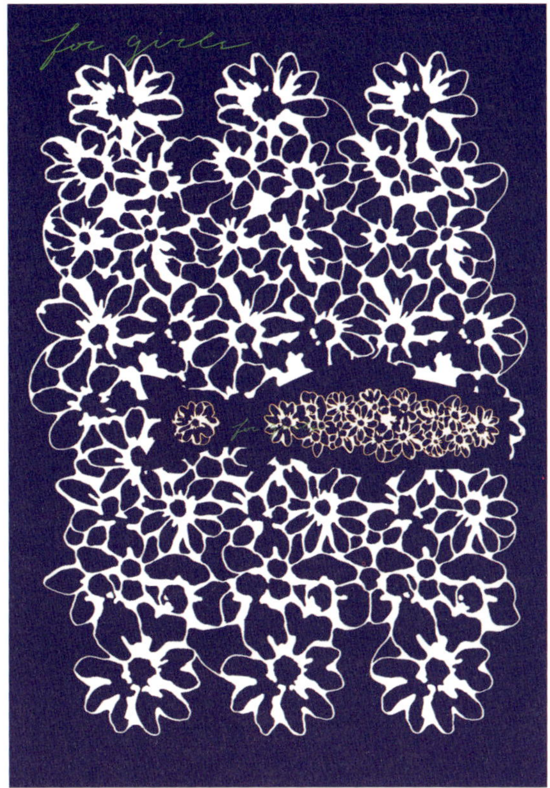

Koinobori Poster

The Gosekku ("five festivals"), which are representative of the four seasons of the year in Japan, originates from China. They have been developed into a unique culture in Japan, of which the Japanese Dragon Boat Festival falls on the fifth day of the fifth month. On this day, carp banners are hung in the gardens of houses to wish growth for the boys. At present, the day has evolved into Children's Day, when people join together to make wishes for boys and girls. As carp banners tend to be atmospheric and majestic in style design, the illustrator tried to get rid of such stereotypes in this project.

Illustrator: Ayaka Shimizu

Tips:

The illustrator breaks stereotypes by using patterns to depict fish scales, hiding the carp banner within them. Color blocks differentiate boundaries, adding amusement.

C75 M0 Y75 K0

C100 M95 Y5 K0

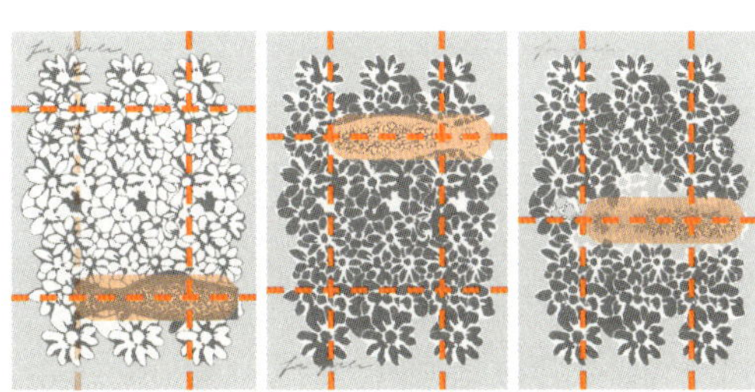

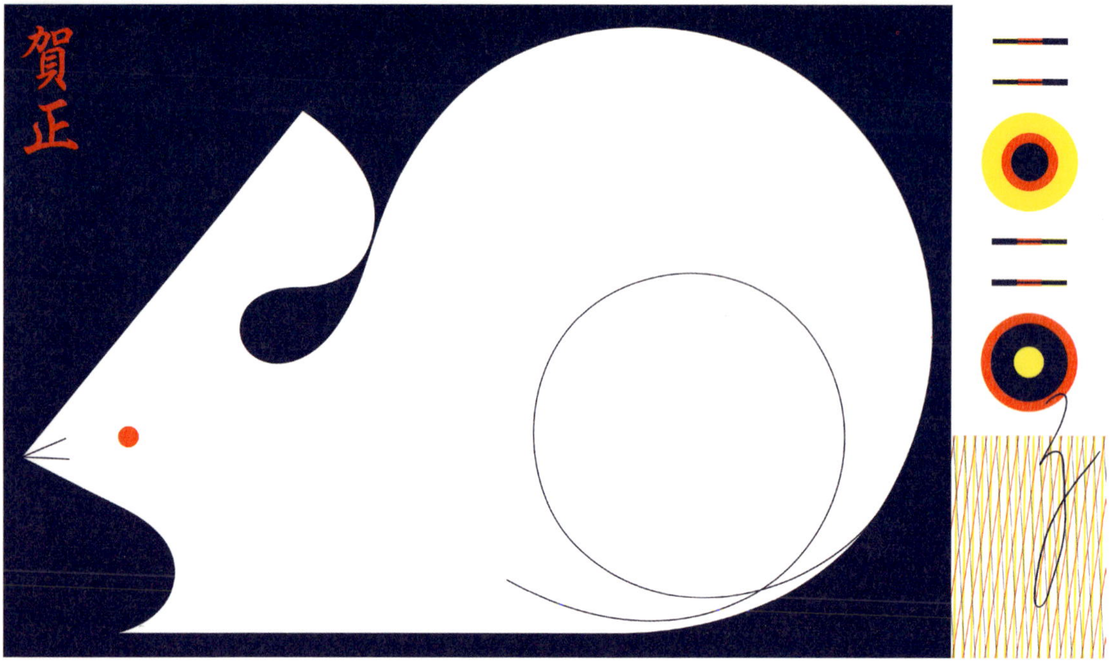

New Year's Card & Goods 2020

This is a New Year's greeting card design for 2020, which is the Year of the Rat in the Chinese zodiac. In addition, the designer also added "crane" and "turtle" images to the card illustration design, both of which reveal meanings of auspice and longevity. The finished product is printed by photolithography. As it differs from the normal way, it creates natural textures on the color blocks, giving the artwork a sense of texture.

Illustrator: Ayaka Shimizu

Tips:

The designer used minimal lines and white space to shape the animals, creating a concise, elegant composition. A special printing technique adds a washed-out effect to the colors, highlighting the traditional aesthetic.

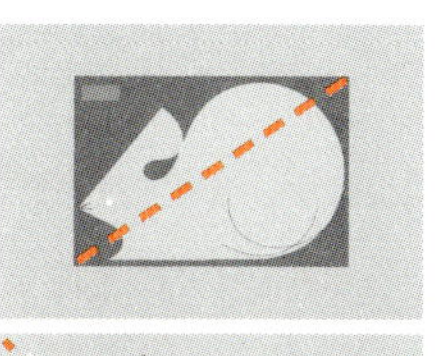

- C0 M90 Y85 K0
- C85 M10 Y100 K10
- C100 M100 Y25 K25

Tips:

Eastern and Western dolls collide and merge cultures through exchanged appearances, fostering a fusion of Eastern and Western traditions.

- C0 M86 Y80 K0
- C0 M15 Y75 K0
- C35 M0 Y24 K0
- C75 M16 Y84 K0
- C69 M15 Y7 K0

From Troublesome Russians to Japanese

The illustrator was asked to create a unique artwork that deviates from conventional perceptions, so she exchanged the appearances of Matryoshka (Russian nesting dolls) and Kokeshi (Japanese wooden dolls).

Illustrator: Masami Ushikubo

Designer: Atsushi Nishitarumi · Chihiro Matsuyama (Krran)

Project Client: Fusosha Inc.

New Year 2021

In 2021, people hoped for the pandemic's end as the new year approached. The world, previously submerged, was slowly recovering. The artwork featured a Kintsugi-repaired vase, symbolizing the Japanese art of fixing pottery with lacquer and precious metals, holding blooming flowers. It expressed hopeful anticipation for a bright new year.

Designer: Josephine Grenier

Tips:

Using "Kintsugi" as a metaphor, it represents the hopeful vision of our world being repaired.

❶

Ryokan OOMURAYA

Jazz Night

2019 1.9 wed

20:30 Start

Bass
Neil Swainson

Guitar
Reg Schwager

Violin
San Murata

Piano
Taiichirou Yamaguchi

Drums
Takashi Sugawara

HAPPY
NEW YEARS
JAZZ LIVE!

Tips:

The texture in the artwork, created by a unique printing technique, exudes a classic and serene charm.

- C1 M27 Y27 K0
- C1 M71 Y68 K0
- C22 M9 Y1 K0
- C85 M51 Y2 K1
- C91 M63 Y12 K43

Works by Yukihira Nagao

❶ *JAZZ NIGHT 2019*: The promotional poster of the jazz music night. ❷ *Ureshino Disco*: The creation was inspired by Artist Andy Warhol.

Illustrator: Yukihira Nagao

❷

Tips:

The traditional Kabuki fan is replaced with a vinyl record, while vibrant red and blue colors create a captivating composition.

- C1 M13 Y9 K0
- C5 M99 Y74 K1
- C30 M100 Y75 K45
- C81 M4 Y47 K1
- C0 M0 Y0 K100

Work by Yuko Shimizu

❶ *Garbage*: This is an album review illustration created by the illustrator for *Rolling Stone* magazine in 2005, featuring the band Garbage's album *Bleed Like Me*. ❷ *Rina Sawayama*: The illustrator designed a conceptual portrait for singer Rina Sawayama's new album *Hold The Girl*. The album's music style combines pop and melancholic folk, so the illustrator wanted to visually represent the singer's various emotions. The portrait features her iconic tattoos on her hands.

Illustrator: Yuko Shimizu

❶

Tips:

Matching droplet shapes lead our gaze from the lead singer to the other band members, adding depth to the composition.

C68 M95 Y99 K75

C25 M89 Y100 K16

C15 M14 Y30 K2

Tips:

The girl's pink flaming hands and hair in the illustration capture the album's theme, enhanced by the striking pink-black contrast.

C35 M98 Y76 K50

C7 M97 Y45 K0

C15 M93 Y14 K0

C5 M22 Y5 K0

❷

❶
日本一

Work by Saki Matsumoto

❶ *Momotaro*: This illustration reimagines the image of Momotaro, the Japanese hero from a folk tale, with a unique art style.
❷ *2020 New Year's Card*: This artwork is a New Year's card created by the illustrator for the Year of the Rat.

Illustrator: Saki Matsumoto

❷

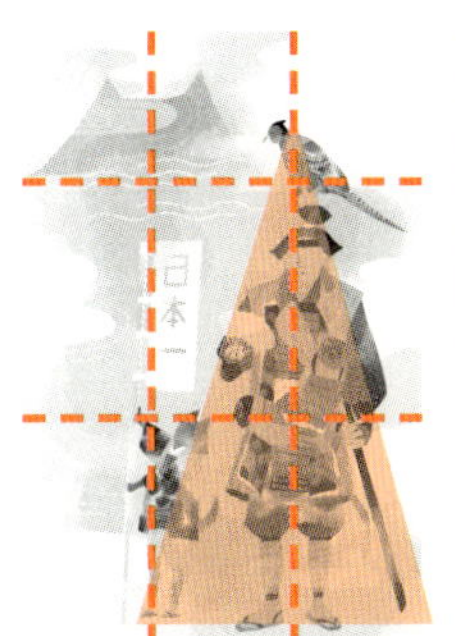

Tips:

❶ The illustrator used geometric collages and watercolor brushstrokes to depict the characters in a fairy tale atmosphere.
❷ Two mice in traditional Japanese yukatas dance joyfully to celebrate the New Year, showcasing detailed and vibrant designs.

C0 M15 Y4 K0	C4 M0 Y24 K0	C12 M0 Y0 K0
C7 M95 Y17 K0	C10 M0 Y82 K0	C33 M1 Y3 K0
C0 M90 Y49 K0	C4 M30 Y86 K0	C95 M92 Y7 K0

Works by Chisato Seino

Illustrator Chisato Seino excels in using colored pencils for her artwork, and these pieces are part of her still-life series.

Illustrator: Chisato Seino

Tips:

Even with ordinary colored pencils, she skillfully captures intricate details.

C33 M20 Y33 K0	C19 M53 Y40 K0
C47 M25 Y69 K0	C33 M65 Y84 K0
C82 M64 Y58 K16	C48 M90 Y80 K11

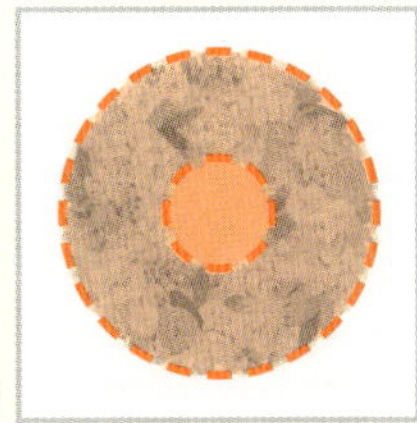

Tips:

By layering colors to create a vintage Riso printing effect, the artwork gains a textured and impactful quality.

- C0 M31 Y31 K5
- C100 M0 Y17 K43
- C0 M79 Y89 K12

Original Works by NINNNNNKI

Ninki's artistic style is based on Riso printing. In this series, various foods become her main subjects, and her bold use of colors adds a unique retro charm to these illustrations.

Illustrator: NINNNNNKI

Solo Exhibition "GOOD BOY, LET'S JOY"

Be intoxicated by what you like, and it will become a sensation throughout the whole world! The theme of the illustrator's solo exhibition is "Being Intoxicated," which is related to his love of beer.

Illustrator: Nori Okawa

Moped Lads Belgian Strong Ale
BEER

Tips:

The bright color palette is both soft and vibrant, while the composition focuses on the main subject as the visual center, highlighting the theme of the "drunken" state.

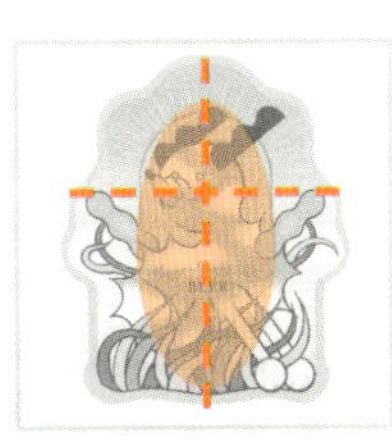

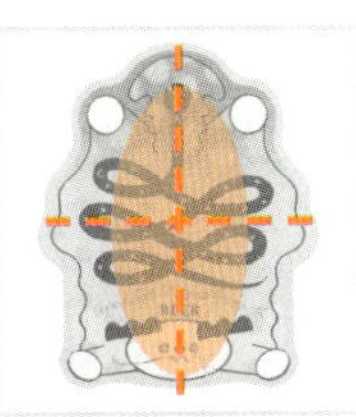

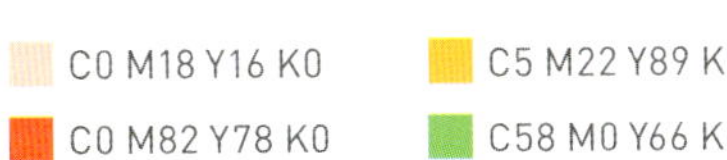

C0 M18 Y16 K0

C0 M82 Y78 K0

C5 M22 Y89 K0

C58 M0 Y66 K0

C65 M0 Y47 K0

C91 M58 Y62 K14

C82 M53 Y0 K0

C0 M0 Y0 K100

Isekado Beer Artist Collaboration

Inspired by beer flavors and concepts, these eye-catching packaging illustrations capture the essence of each brew. March's "In Your Life" shows an excited beer-induced cell morphing into flowers, while April's "Honkaku IPA" features a majestic lion with traditional elements symbolizing Isekado's 25th anniversary.

Illustrator: Nori Okawa

Client: Niken Chaya Mochi Kadoya Honten Co.

Tips:

These beer label illustrations are visually engaging with exaggerated and vibrant depictions, appealing to young audience.

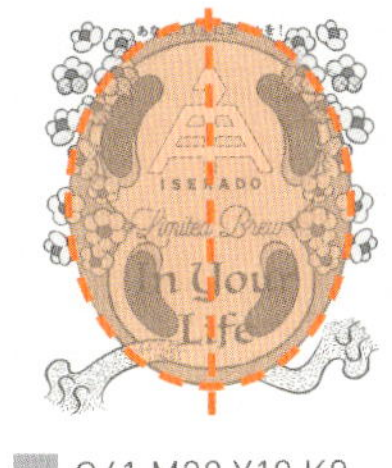

C2 M19 Y16 K0
C9 M91 Y93 K0
C4 M6 Y13 K0
C5 M22 Y88 K0
C41 M29 Y19 K0
C27 M40 Y97 K0
C73 M11 Y29 K0
C91 M59 Y72 K24

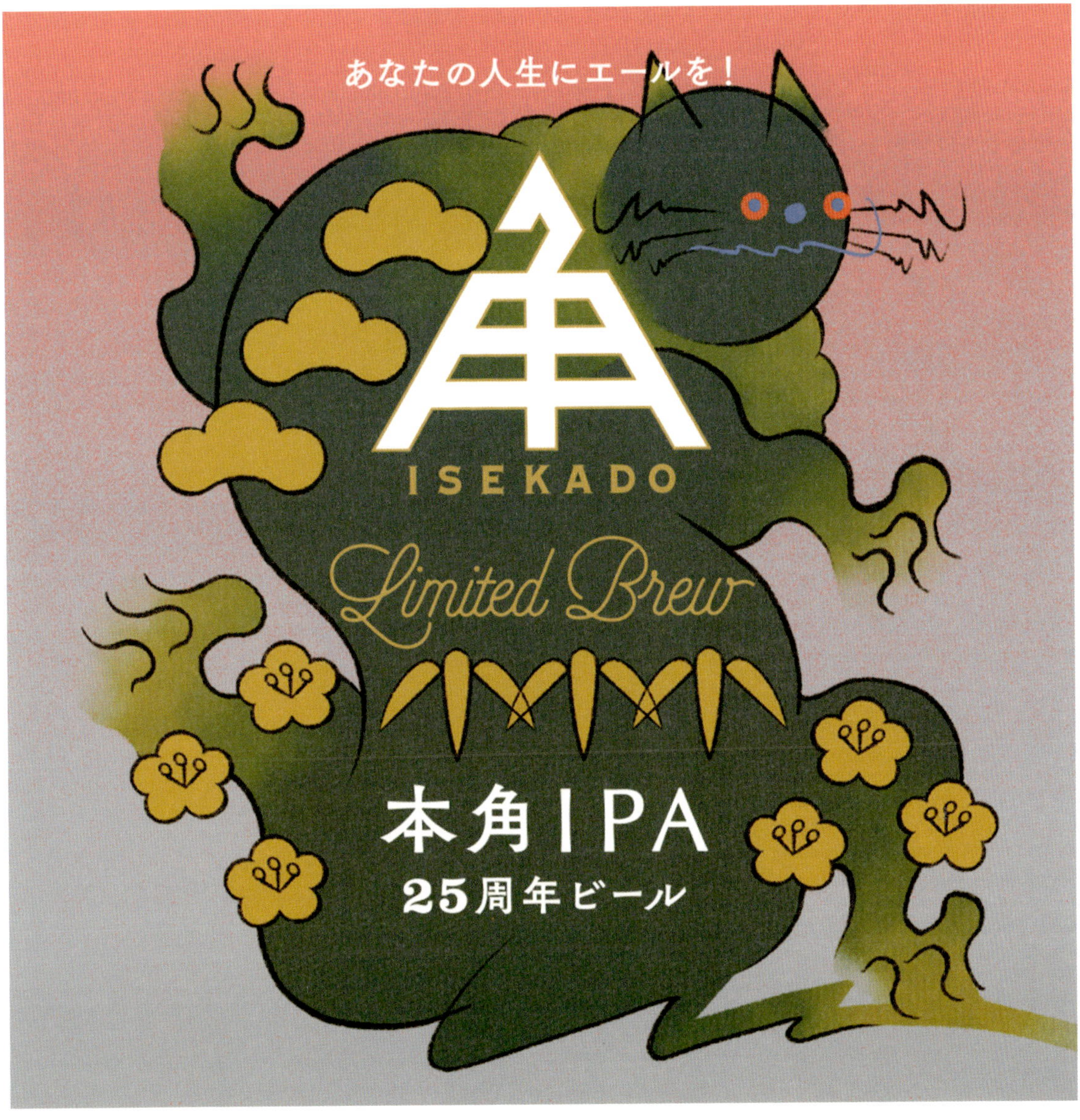

あなたの人生にエールを！

ISEKADO

Limited Brew

本角IPA

25周年ビール

❶ Works by Nori Okawa

❶ *P.T.A (Park Trade Association)*: The illustrator's vibrant artwork captures a festive atmosphere for the event. ❷ *I'M POSSIBLE*: The exhibition theme of "I'm Possible" is represented by a tiger emerging from a folded screen, embodying the spirit of the Japanese folk character "ikkyu."

Illustrator: Nori Okawa

Tips:

❶ Strong lines and patterns merge traditional Japanese aesthetics with modern techniques, creating a vibrant artwork.
❷ The illustrator transforms the image of the "tiger" with bold colors and graphic elements, capturing the essence of a distinctive traditional tale.

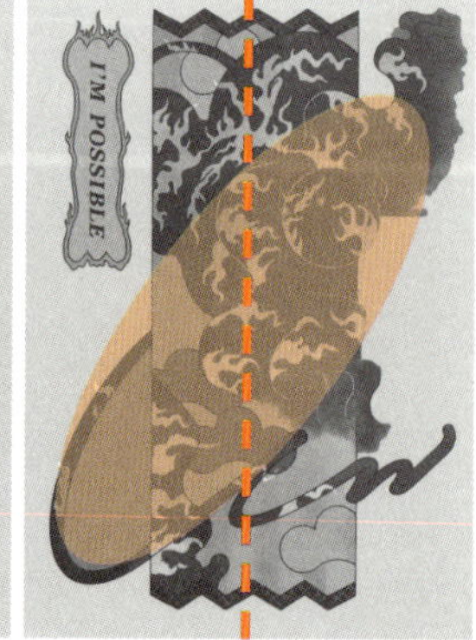

2
I'M POSSIBLE

Series by Koromochi Nakamura

Works ❶—❼ were created for an exhibition. It is evident that the illustrator pays great attention to "coincidences" during the creative process, often depict unrealistic and irrational elements. However, it is precisely these unconventional elements that make her works intriguing. Works ❽—❿ were other personal creations by the illustrator.

Illustrator: Koromochi Nakamura

❼

Tips:

Casual drawings of unconventional things bring unique experiences and unexpected surprises.

- C4 M35 Y19 K0
- C4 M54 Y91 K0
- C68 M25 Y42 K0
- C47 M0 Y16 K0
- C90 M67 Y9 K0
- C76 M50 Y50 K65

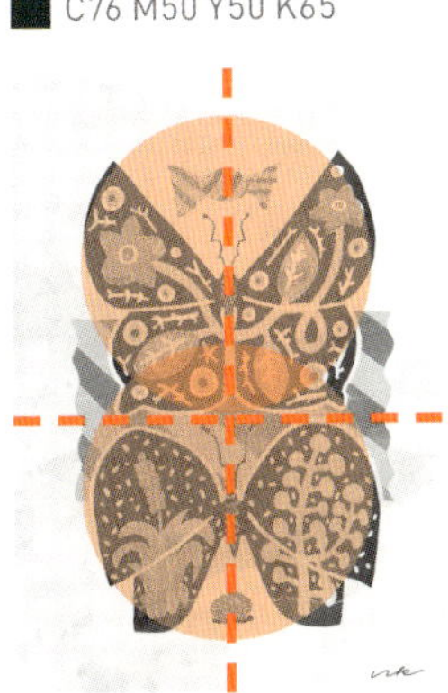

❾

❿

Original Works by Yuka Hiiragi

These illustrations are for a 2023 calendar, featuring plants of different seasons creatively depicted with animals for joy.

Illustrator: Yuka Hiiragi

Tips:

This acrylic gouache series has a textured effect based on delicate depiction, giving a soft and soothing appearance.

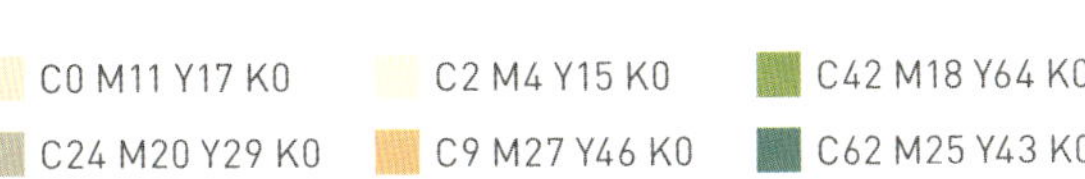

C0 M11 Y17 K0
C2 M4 Y15 K0
C42 M18 Y64 K0
C24 M20 Y29 K0
C9 M27 Y46 K0
C62 M25 Y43 K0

Sonepon Original Illustrations

This set of illustrations is a collection of practice works by the illustrator Sonepon, who often focuses on nighttime scenes and enjoys depicting scenes from her dreams.

Illustrator: Sonepon

Tips:

The brushstrokes and colors portray the illustrator's dream-like scenes, capturing the serenity and loneliness of the night through light and shadow.

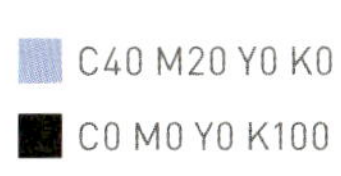

C10 M72 Y93 K0

C8 M4 Y25 K0

C40 M20 Y0 K0

C0 M0 Y0 K100

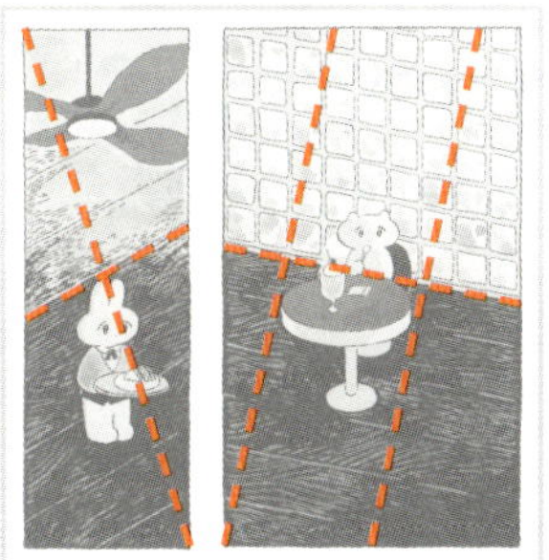

シンプルであるということ：多様であること、豊かであること。

What We Talk About When We Talk About Simplicity: Colorful and All-encompassing.

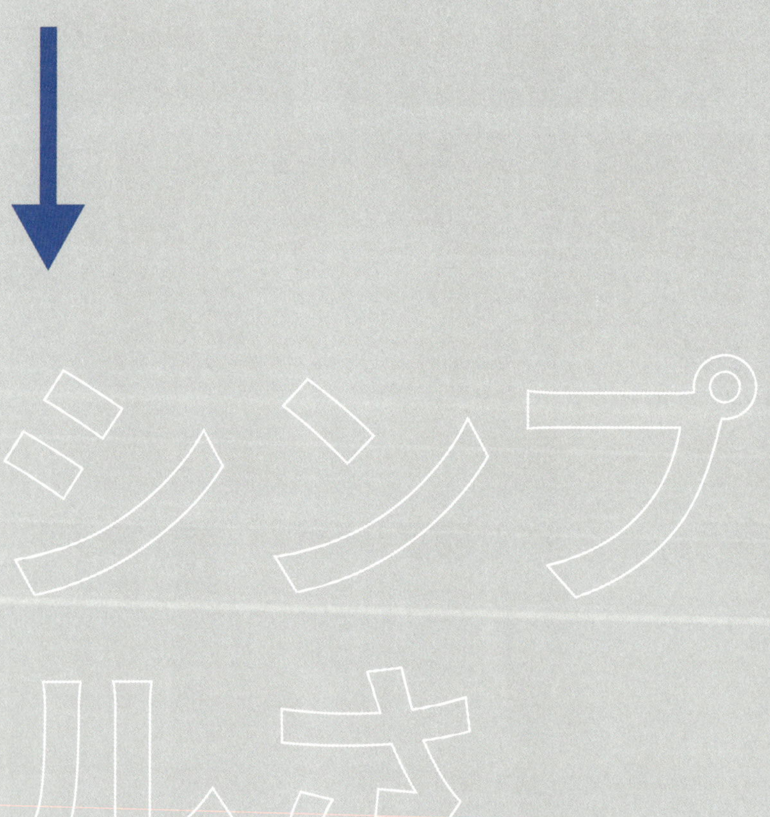

Tips:

These illustrations capture the beauty of everyday life with their detailed hand-drawn style, conveying a sense of authenticity and emotion to the viewers.

- C0 M68 Y68 K0
- C0 M30 Y57 K0
- C70 M0 Y60 K0
- C83 M55 Y0 K0
- C0 M0 Y0 K20
- C0 M0 Y0 K100

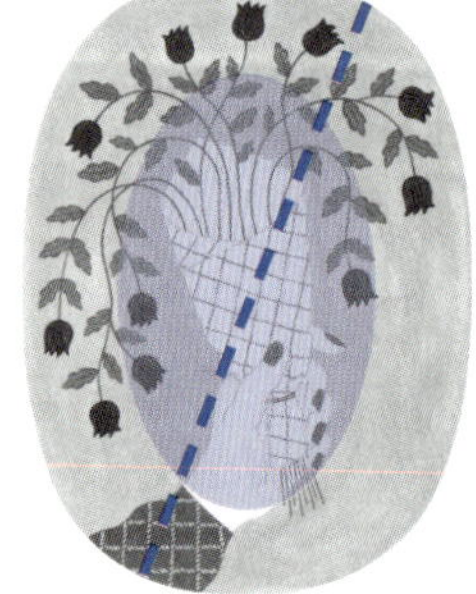

ONE SCENE

This series of illustrations focuses on depicting some hand movements and gestures, such as holding flowers or petting animals.

Illustrator: Hama Yoshie

BUTTER SCOTCH

Summer Flower Garden

The designer incorporates summer vibes into the packaging design, evoking joy and delight in candy lovers as they feel immersed in a vibrant flower field. The soothing illustration style creates a cozy and friendly design.

Designer: Yui Okumura

Client: Bairindou Co.,Ltd.

Tips:

Using a low saturation color palette creates a summer atmosphere.

- C0 M50 Y0 K0
- C2 M0 Y80 K0
- C63 M8 Y25 K0
- C56 M9 Y62 K0
- C80 M8 Y71 K11
- C67 M28 Y0 K0
- C84 M47 Y16 K0
- C0 M0 Y0 K25

MILKHALL Little Envelope

This set of envelopes are designed for the antique store MILKHALL. It is a combination of pop color schemes and funny graphics.

Designer: Agata Yamaguchi

Design Agency: collé inc.

Tips:

The vibrant colors and simple graphics harmonize perfectly, enhancing the childlike innocence of these slightly "clumsy" illustrations.

- C27 M98 Y86 K0
- C11 M66 Y59 K0
- C8 M9 Y76 K0
- C76 M11 Y55 K0
- C76 M21 Y13 K0
- C33 M41 Y56 K0

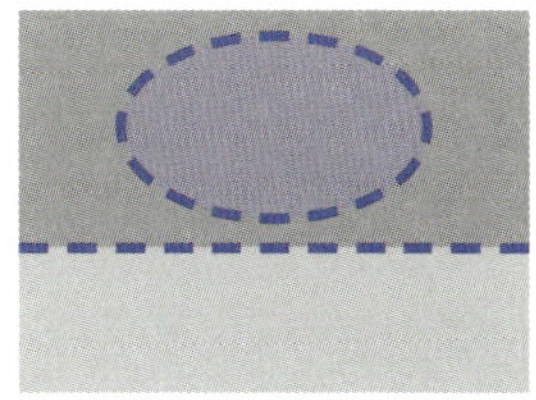

D-BROS New Year Greeting Card

With just a few colorful and simple blocks, fascinating animal and plant patterns are formed. These greeting cards exude a playful and childlike sense of wonder.

Design Studio: DRAFT
Creative Director: Satoru Miyata
Art Director: Eriko Kawakami

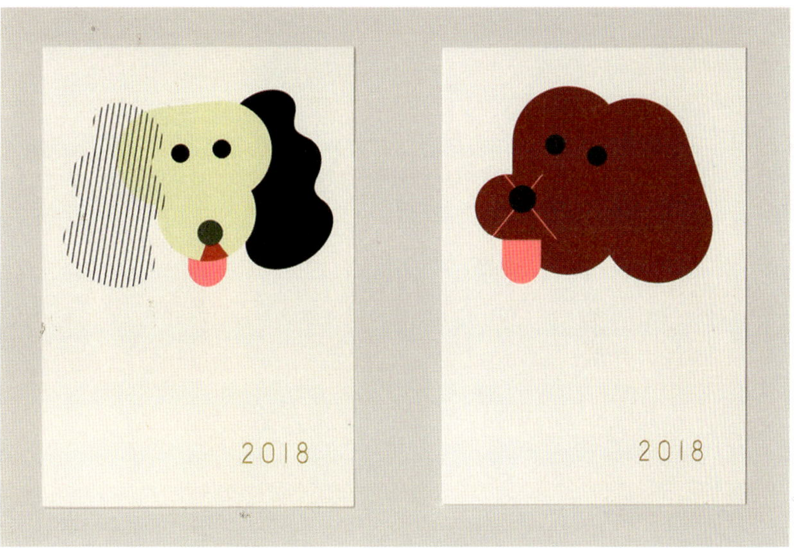

Tips:

The designer captures the essence of animals' appearance and movements in a modern and innovative graphic style.

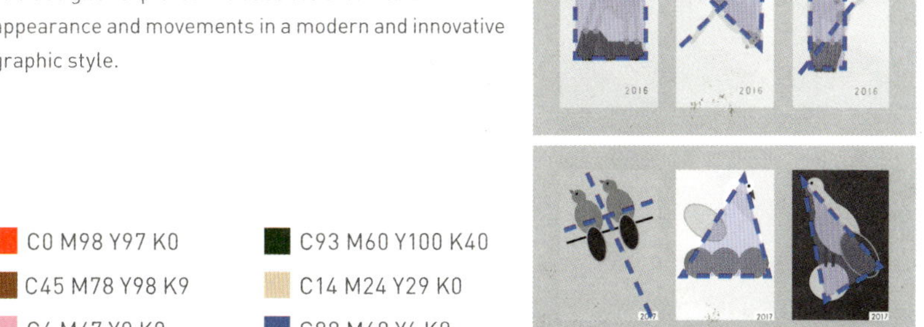

- C0 M98 Y97 K0
- C45 M78 Y98 K9
- C6 M47 Y0 K0
- C93 M60 Y100 K40
- C14 M24 Y29 K0
- C88 M60 Y6 K0

❶

❷

Tips:

The illustrator captures the elegant postures of dancers through varied curves, showcasing the soft and gentle beauty of the human body.

- C0 M20 Y9 K0
- C1 M29 Y100 K0
- C36 M80 Y100 K49
- C89 M55 Y69 K60
- C74 M36 Y0 K0
- C100 M96 Y25 K16

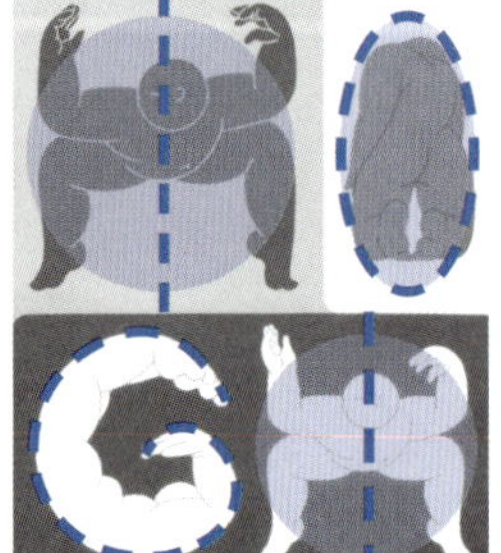

Works by Mameko Maeda

❶ *Earth Energy, Mind's Eye*: A collaboration between FAVORRIC and the artist, this canvas bag represents the concept of "feeling Earth's energy through meditation."
❷ *HIGH*: Exhibited at the artist's "Choreographica" solo exhibition in 2022, this artwork portrays the graceful curves and postures of dancing bodies.
❸ *Tote Bag*: Soft palm patterns contrast with the transparent plastic bag's subtle folds.
❹ *M*: The illustrator captures a fleeting moment in a dance, sparking viewers' imagination about the subsequent actions.

Illustrator: Mameko Maeda

❸

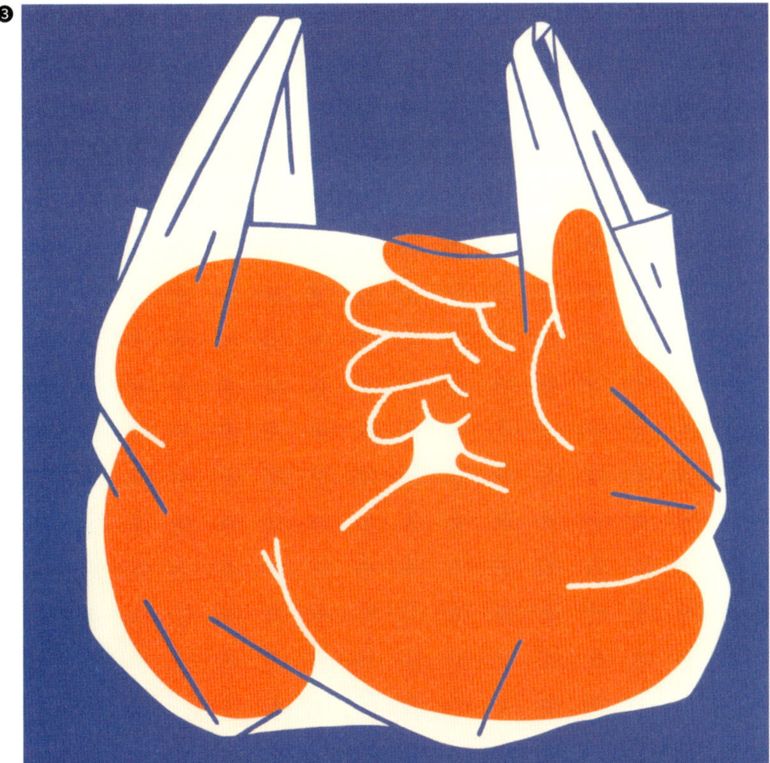

❹

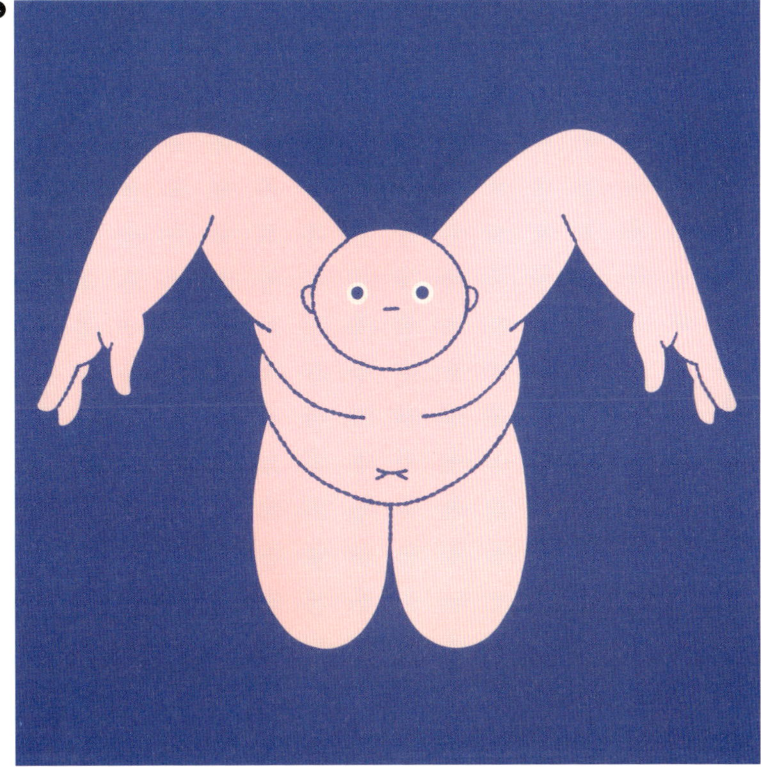

Tokyo Zokei University 2022

The designers use everyday objects and common scenes as their creative inspiration. Their goal is to convey a positive message to upcoming university students, emphasizing that life is filled with beauty.

Designers: Taki Uesugi, Saki Uesugi

Project Client: Tokyo Zokei University

Tips:

The designers deconstruct and reimagine everyday objects, filling them with vibrant colors to create healing illustrations. These illustrations convey a positive outlook on life and offer encouragement.

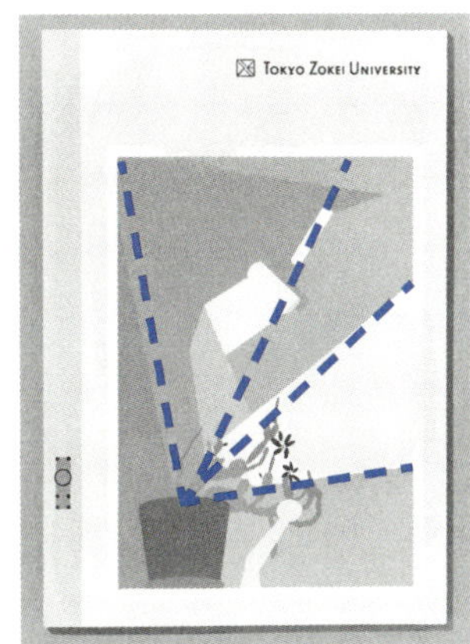

Okinawa Yakult 60th Anniversary

This packaging design celebrates the 60th anniversary of the Okinawa "Yakult" brand. The poster features 60 personified bottles in a parade formation, expressing gratitude to the people of Okinawa.

Designers: Aya Codama, Ryoya Yamazaki

Project Client: Yakult Okinawa Co., Ltd.

Tips:

The designers give a human touch to the Yakult bottles, using creative compositions, expressions, and patterns on their small surfaces to add a sense of fun and creativity.

C0 M90 Y85 K0

C0 M80 Y95 K0

C55 M30 Y10 K0

C50 M70 Y80 K70

C0 M35 Y85 K0

C0 M0 Y0 K0

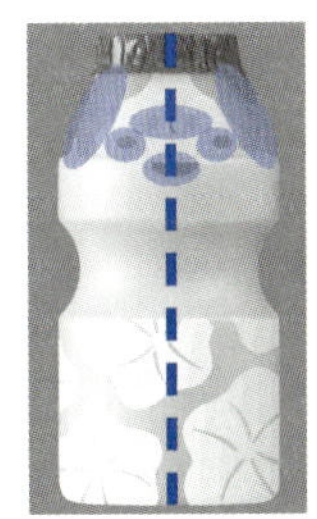

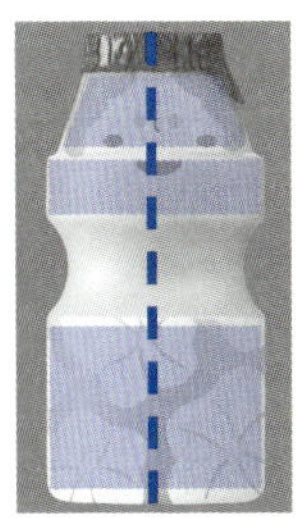

Tips:

The illustrator employs adjacent colors, creating a gentle and warm ambiance that exudes a healing touch.

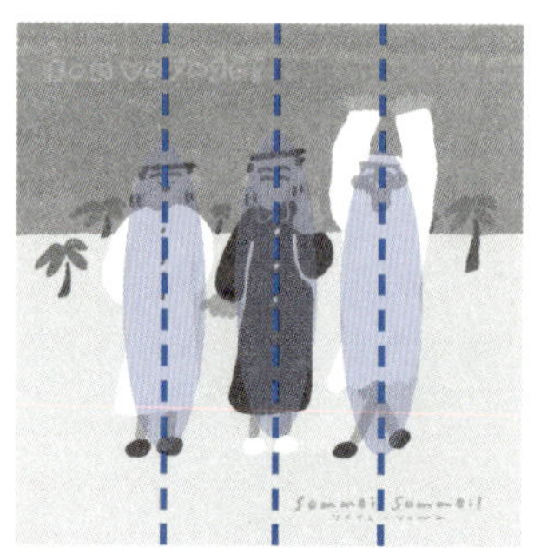

- C9 M60 Y63 K0
- C2 M7 Y75 K0
- C51 M7 Y60 K0
- C74 M42 Y62 K0

Client Works by Misaki Nakamura

The "clumsy" lines and color blocks, along with the "flat-topped" characters, embody the artistic style of this illustrator.

Illustrator: Misaki Nakamura

Client: ❶ Umi Shizukuda, SOWASOWA RECORDS ❷ YAMATO Co., Ltd. ❸ *TEMPURA* magazine
❹ Magazine House Co., Ltd. ❺ Eri Tobita, DENEN ONGAKUSHITSU ❻ Akane Inoue, PARK GALLERY

❷

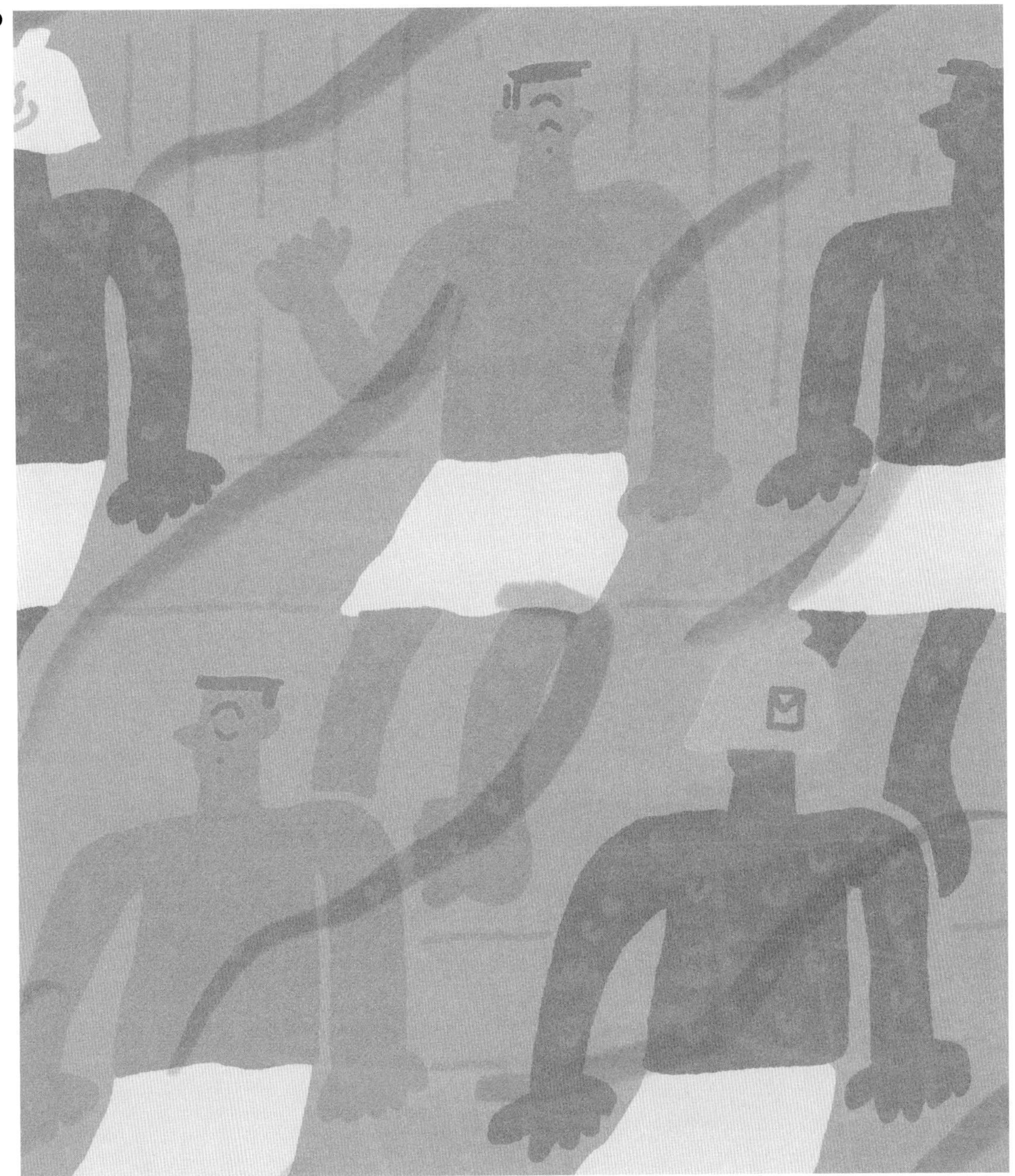

❹
わたしのお取り寄せ
WATASHI NO OTORIYOSE
❺
田園音楽室
vol.2
❻

Cover for *Yamagata Life Real Voices*

This is the cover designed for the booklet *"Authentic Voices of Yamagata Life,"* featuring stories of immigrants in Yamagata City. With a childlike art style, the illustrator portrays the newcomers and the city's landscapes, capturing the allure and enjoyment of life in Yamagata.

Illustrator: Nakayama Shinichi

Yamagata Life
Real Voices

山形のまちに飛びこんで
暮らしてわかる色々なこと

リアルローカル山形 編集

Tips:

The artwork features varied color blocks representing mountains, sun, sky, and land. Arranged unevenly, they form a complete and vibrant composition.

- C0 M76 Y83 K0
- C27 M70 Y83 K12
- C75 M20 Y75 K0
- C71 M41 Y11 K0
- C14 M15 Y22 K0

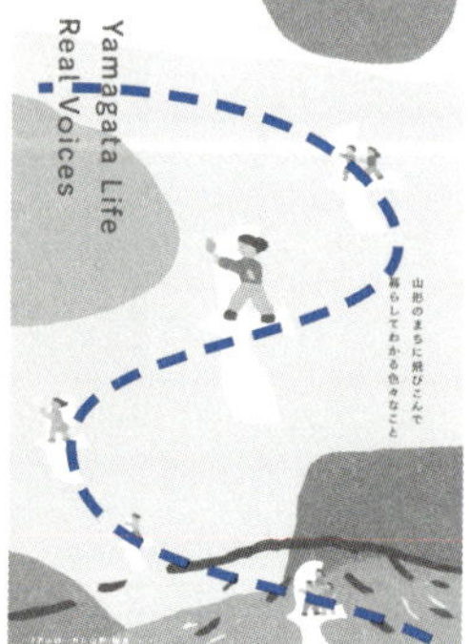

Cover for *Sunset Sunrise*

As the sun sets, casting a colorful glow, the illustrator captures a scene of the characters engrossed in admiring the evening sky, accompanied by the soothing fragrance of flowers and trees.

Illustrator: Nakayama Shinichi **Publisher:** Kodansha **Writter:** Shuhei Nire

Tips:

The illustrator's three-part composition evenly depicts the sunset, expansive sea, and a couple on the shore during twilight, creating a serene and delightful ambiance.

- C3 M25 Y68 K0
- C53 M73 Y82 K18
- C89 M53 Y81 K19
- C77 M34 Y11 K0
- C56 M41 Y36 K0

日常雑貨と
非日常雑貨
日常と非日常
Nichijo to Hinichijo
Antique Furniture
Brocante
Select Item
16 →
AU 18
JUIN 2021
AM12 PM7
SUPREY
26-1 Gikurintani
Chikujo-machi,
Chikujo-gun, Fukuoka-ken
812-0978 Japan
Quotidien et
extraordinaire
https://www.instagram.com/brindle_brindle/

Quotidien et Extraordinaire

In this series, the designer creatively reimagines ordinary daily scenes, showcasing experimentation and innovation. From a sushi conveyor belt resembling a hovering UFO to a hat transforming into a turtle on one's head, and a posture resembling lying on a crocodile while driving, the artworks blur the distinction between everyday scenes and imaginative concepts.

Designer: Agata Yamaguchi

Design Agency: collé inc.

Tips:

Using the same composition but with different elements and color schemes, contrasting effects are achieved.

C31 M96 Y76 K0

C10 M76 Y76 K0

C10 M4 Y87 K0

C56 M42 Y34 K0

C90 M53 Y100 K23

C71 M31 Y15 K0

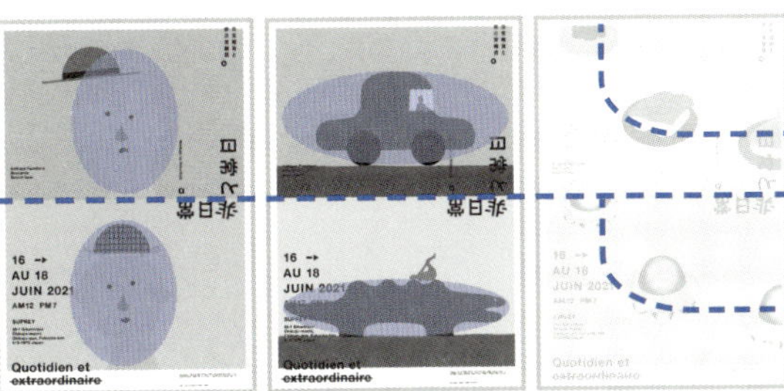

How to eat delicious Sandwich Toasted Bread

365日
と
食パン

Tips:

Yellow with high saturation is used as the main color, and the hand-painted strokes highlight the childishness.

C0 M94 Y98 K0	C62 M18 Y17 K0
C4 M0 Y83 K0	C91 M66 Y0 K0

365 NICHI&WHITE BREAD

The illustrator captures everyday life scenes of girls and boys, conveying the message of enjoying bread without hesitation in various days and scenarios, showcasing the brand name of the bakery, 365.

Illustrator: Keiko Shibata
Graphic Designer: Satoru Nakaichi
Art Directors: Koichi Tamamura, Satoru Nakaichi
Design Agency: LIGHTS DESIGN
Project Client: ULTRA KITCHEN

Talk

This is the material for the designer's solo exhibition themed "Talk." Prior to this, the designer conducted interviews with individuals of different genders, ages, and professions, and created portraits of them.

Designer: Agata Yamaguchi

Design Agency: collé inc.

Tips:

Using simple color blocks, the illustrator captures the expressions and postures of the characters, creating a strikingly captivating and abstract representation.

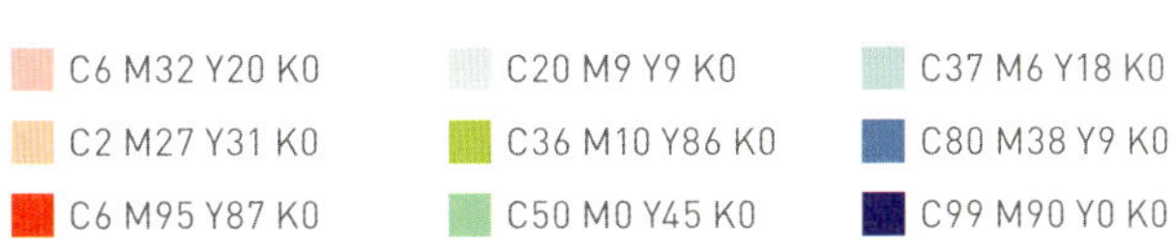

尼彦

Tips:

To Portray traditional cultural imagery with a modern twist, featuring cute and amusing characters in vibrant colors.

- C0 M98 Y84 K0
- C70 M96 Y94 K69
- C10 M0 Y83 K0
- C69 M0 Y54 K0
- C90 M61 Y43 K2
- C80 M63 Y0 K0
- C18 M60 Y0 K0
- C78 M91 Y5 K0

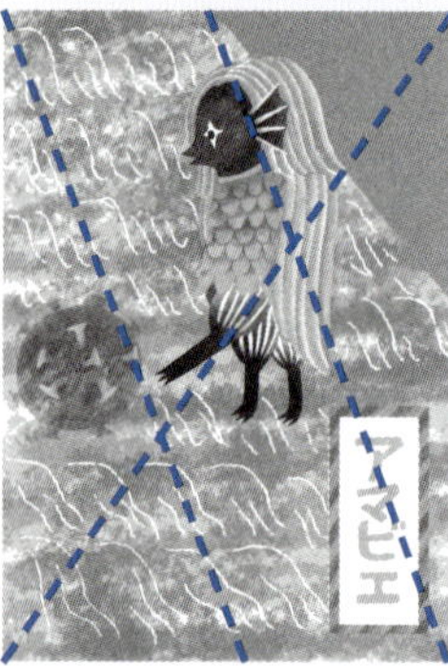

Amabie and Amabiko

During the COVID-19 pandemic, the illustrator depicted Amabie and Amabiko, ancient Japanese symbols believed to conquer epidemics, as a hopeful prayer for a return to normalcy in life.

Illustrator: Saki Matsumoto

アマビエ

Okada&Ryo babaroa Manpuku

2022.02.12SAT at Shimokitazawa BASEMENTBAR OPEN 12:00 START 12:30

TICKET ¥2,000+D FOOD: Curry Sha RESERVE: okaryo.com/oyatsu-time

OYATSU TIME

Those posters were created by the illustrator for the event "OYATSU TIME." "OYATSU TIME" refers to the "snack time" in the afternoon, around 3 o'clock.

Illustrator: Tasuku Komatsu

Tips:

Bright and vibrant colors, combined with playful IP character designs.

- C7 M83 Y72 K0
- C11 M10 Y67 K0
- C60 M21 Y4 K0
- C81 M72 Y0 K0

Works by Miho Miyauchi: Girl's Daily Life

The illustrator aims to express through this series of illustrations: "Love yourself and live on your own terms."

Illustrator: Miho Miyauchi

Tips:

The illustrator's carefree and effortless linework is perfect for merchandise development.

C0 M33 Y59 K0

C3 M25 Y17 K0

C24 M2 Y10 K0

C78 M51 Y4 K2

SUPER STAR

Tips:

Creating a vibrant and playful design by arranging smiling faces into the number "55."

- C0 M100 Y100 K0
- C0 M65 Y65 K0
- C0 M0 Y87 K0
- C0 M46 Y70 K53
- C66 M0 Y79 K39
- C75 M45 Y0 K30

MBS Radio *Youth Town* 55th Anniversary Logo

This logo is designed for MBS Radio's 55th anniversary program *Young Town*, featuring smiling faces of listeners forming the number "55."

Illustrator: Peko Asano
Project Client: MBS Radio

PIZZA BEAR

This packaging is designed for the food brand Mary's, featuring the main character, the "Pizza-eating Bear."

Designer: Atsushi Hirano

Design Studio: AFFORDANCE inc.

Tips:

The dynamic, adorable, and colorful lines vividly depict the image of the "Pizza-eating Bear."

- C5 M96 Y100 K0
- C23 M73 Y91 K11
- C8 M16 Y98 K0
- C82 M16 Y100 K2
- C83 M54 Y38 K16
- C0 M0 Y0 K35

PIZZA BEAR
p
p
PIZZA BEAR
p
Delicious
Cookies
20 Pieces
PIZZA BEAR
p
Delicious
Cookies
36 Pieces

PIZZA BEAR
p
p

Works by Seiji Matsumoto

❶ *SEIJI MATSUMOTO EXHIBITION "EVERYDAY"*: This artwork is the main visual for the solo exhibition "EVERYDAY" at YUKIKOMIZUTANI in Tokyo, expressing the beauty of our daily lives. ❷ *"Fun!"*: These artworks depict the fun-filled daily lives of the "ANDY THE MOUSE" and aim to bring joy to viewers at the "Fun!" art exhibition in Osaka.

Illustrator: Seiji Matsumoto

❶

❷

Tips:

The abstract background contrasts vividly with the concrete "little mice" formed by the lines, offering viewers a unique visual experience.

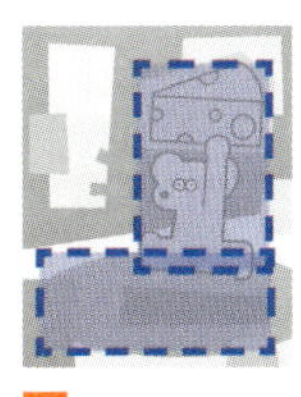

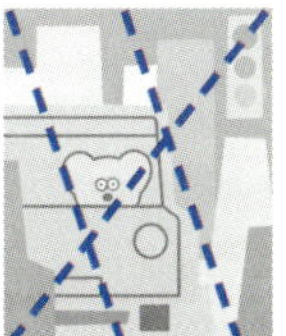

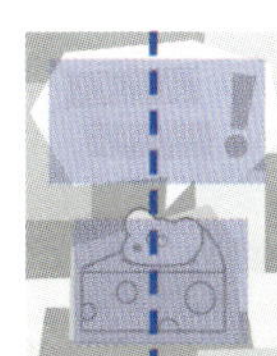

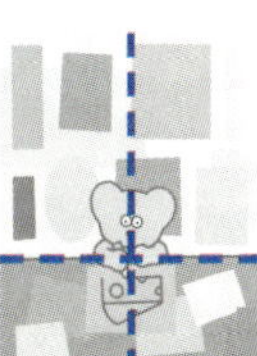

C0 M72 Y82 K0
C48 M85 Y100 K19
C0 M5 Y98 K0
C0 M29 Y4 K0
C47 M13 Y2 K0
C66 M43 Y0 K2
C37 M41 Y0 K0
C88 M77 Y0 K0
C82 M11 Y88 K1
C90 M35 Y75 K18
C0 M0 Y0 K17
C0 M0 Y0 K30

Works by Ryotaro Hirosaki

❶ A gift card designed for Valentine's Day, emphasizing the importance of heartfelt sentiment over outward appearance. ❷ A minimalist and innovative flower-themed poster created using a single line. ❸ This artwork combines a dignified tone with refracted light and flowing curves, evoking a feeling of freedom and relaxation. ❹ In this poster, the designer maintains their style by abstracting individual flower outlines and connecting them with curves to form a bouquet.

Designer: Ryotaro Hirosaki

Tips:

Smooth lines intertwine and fill with red, outlining the passionate emotions within a lover's heart.

C15 M100 Y100 K0   C0 M0 Y0 K30

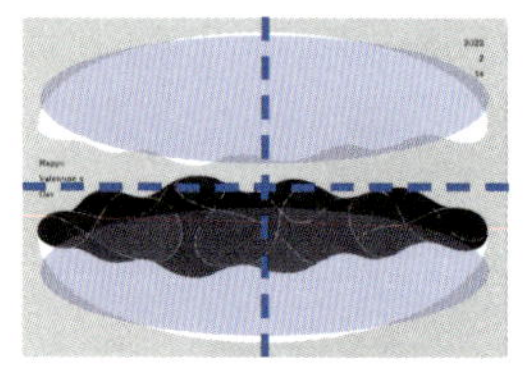

The graceful curves abstractly depict the exquisite posture of each blooming flower.

C20 M0 Y90 K0

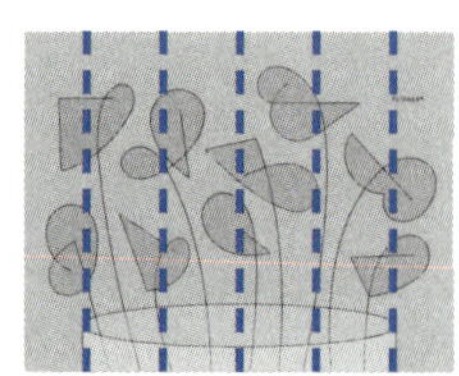

❷

❸

❹

Temiyage From Noborito

This is the packaging design for a coffee stall in Noborito, a suburb near Tokyo.

Designer: Yuta Miura

Project Client: Ribot Coffee Roasters

Tips:

Simple curves and shapes create casual and comfortable floral patterns.

- C7 M98 Y76 K0
- C10 M27 Y53 K0
- C40 M53 Y98 K19
- C94 M37 Y87 K30
- C92 M34 Y36 K5
- C0 M0 Y0 K35

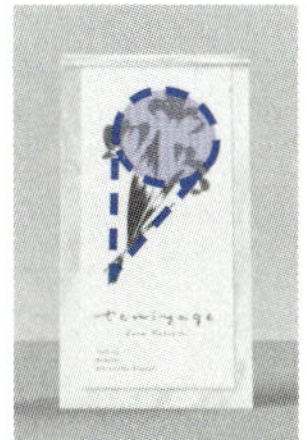

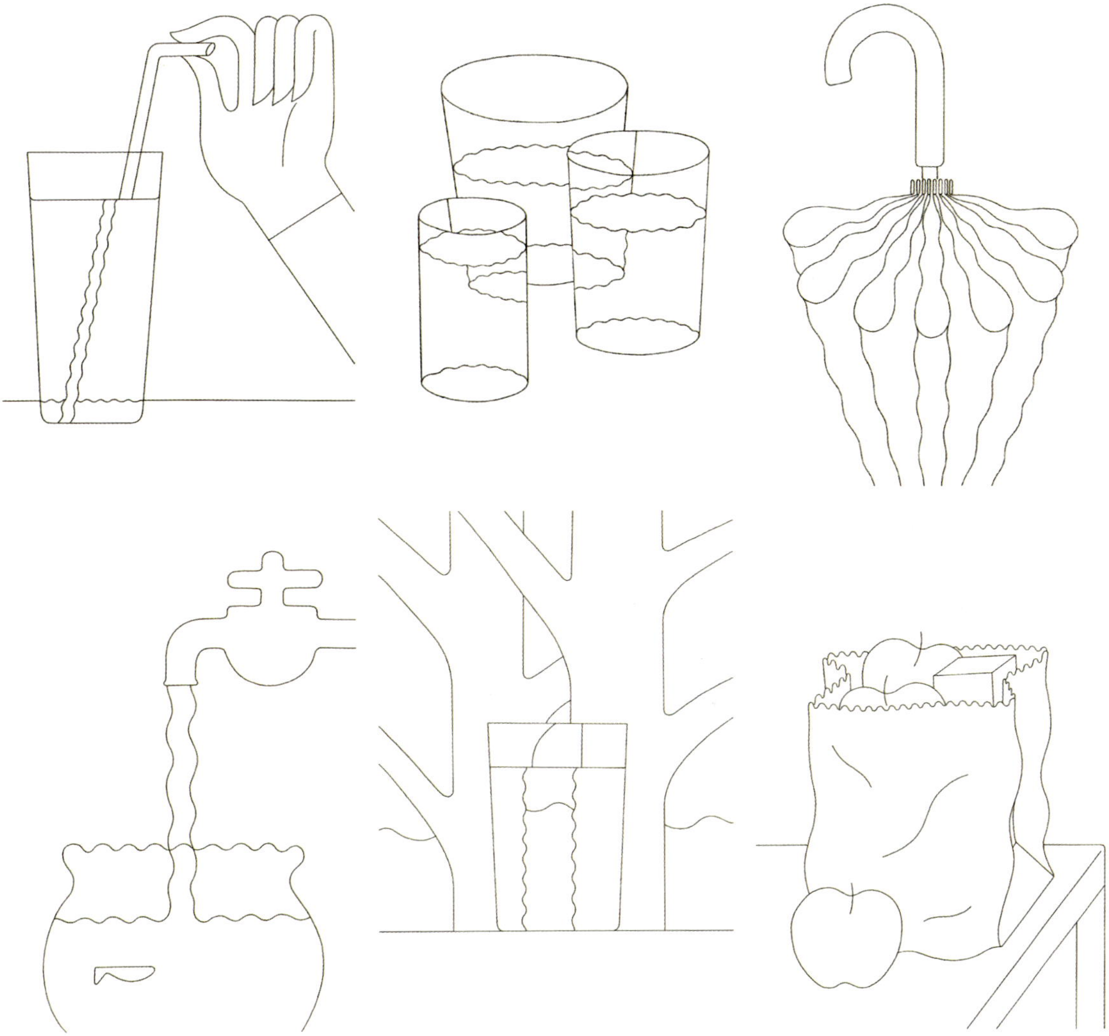

Works by Chiaki Kobayashi

The illustrator use ordinary scenes and familiar objects as motifs for her illustrations, which are mainly simplified drawings with simple, single lines reminiscent of computer graphics. The illustrator draw wavy lines in her works, indicating that both the world and everyone'self are ever-changing entities.

Illustrator: Chiaki Kobayashi

Tips:

Using wavy lines in still life sketches accentuates object states, creating movement within stillness.

- C0 M0 Y100 K0
- C0 M0 Y0 K100

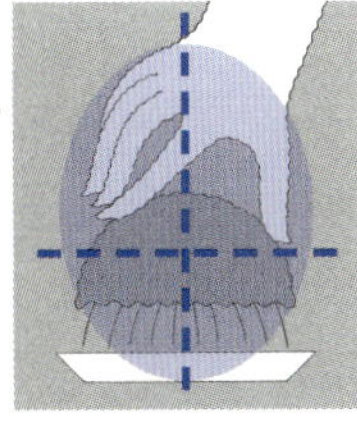

1

THINK DEEPLY

KEEP THINKING TO FIND
THE BEST WAY TO EXPRESS YOURSELF
THROUGH ART: IF IT IS BETTER
TO TRUST YOUR FEELINGS,
IF YOU SHOULD MAKE A CAREFUL PLAN
OR IF IT IS BEST TO KEEP IT SIMPLE.

武蔵野美術学院

TOKYO MUSASHINO ACADEMY OF ART

A series of posters designed for the Musashino Art University in Tokyo.

Designer: Agata Yamaguchi

Design Agency: collé inc.

Tips: Randomly combining shapes of different colors, it exhibits rich artistic qualities.

C80 M23 Y92 K0	C7 M4 Y86 K0
C4 M6 Y15 K0	C81 M44 Y11 K0
C18 M42 Y80 K0	C0 M0 Y0 K70
C11 M95 Y64 K0	C0 M0 Y0 K100

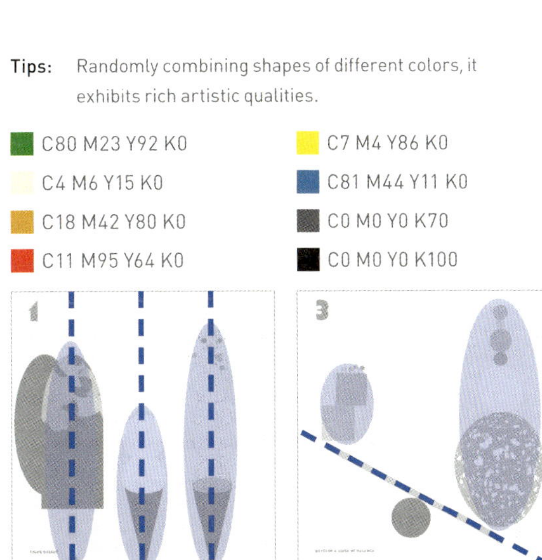

Lie Encyclopedia

These blurred and fabricated plants are products of the illustrator's imagination. Within these depicted plants, the states of fracture and withering are portrayed, indicating that various states of plants can possess their own allure.

Illustrator: Takuya Kawaguchi

Tips:

The stems of the plants are bent and broken, serving to divide the composition; two flower buds echo each other, forming the visual centerpiece of the artwork.

■ C0 M0 Y0 K100

POLARIS

This series of artworks combines constellations, mythology, and serene animal scenes, evoking a sense of peace and healing.

Illustrator: Hama Yoshie

Tips:

Solid backgrounds, specific palettes, and varied subjects create a harmonious and healing illustration series.

- C0 M80 Y100 K0
- C0 M36 Y100 K0
- C82 M4 Y91 K0
- C100 M80 Y0 K0
- C19 M4 Y4 K0
- C0 M0 Y0 K100

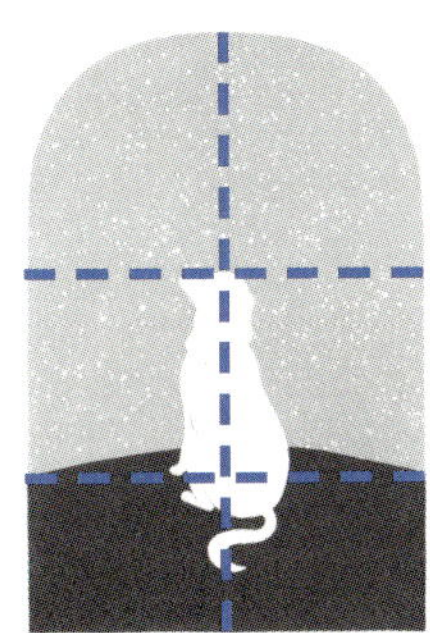

What Modernity Tastes Like?

モダンな

Daily Color Compositions

Tomomi excels at using basic shapes and vibrant colors to create illustrations with a strong personal style. She finds each drawing process to be a novel experience and aims to bring joy and relief to viewers from everyday life through her simple and enjoyable artwork.

Illustrator: Tomomi Mizukoshi

Tips:

By graphically depicting everyday life scenes, the illustrator offers a unique aesthetic experience through humorous, formal, and well-composed art, redefining the ordinary in an extraordinary way.

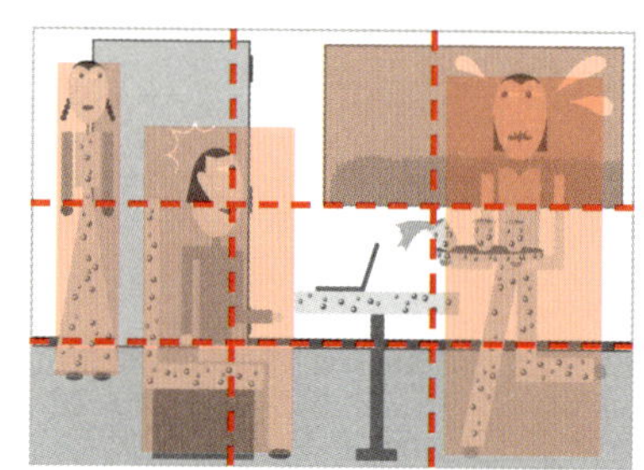

C0 M100 Y100 K0

C0 M38 Y0 K0

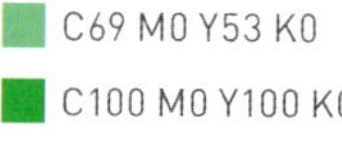

C69 M0 Y53 K0

C100 M0 Y100 K0

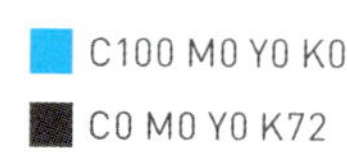

C100 M0 Y0 K0

C0 M0 Y0 K72

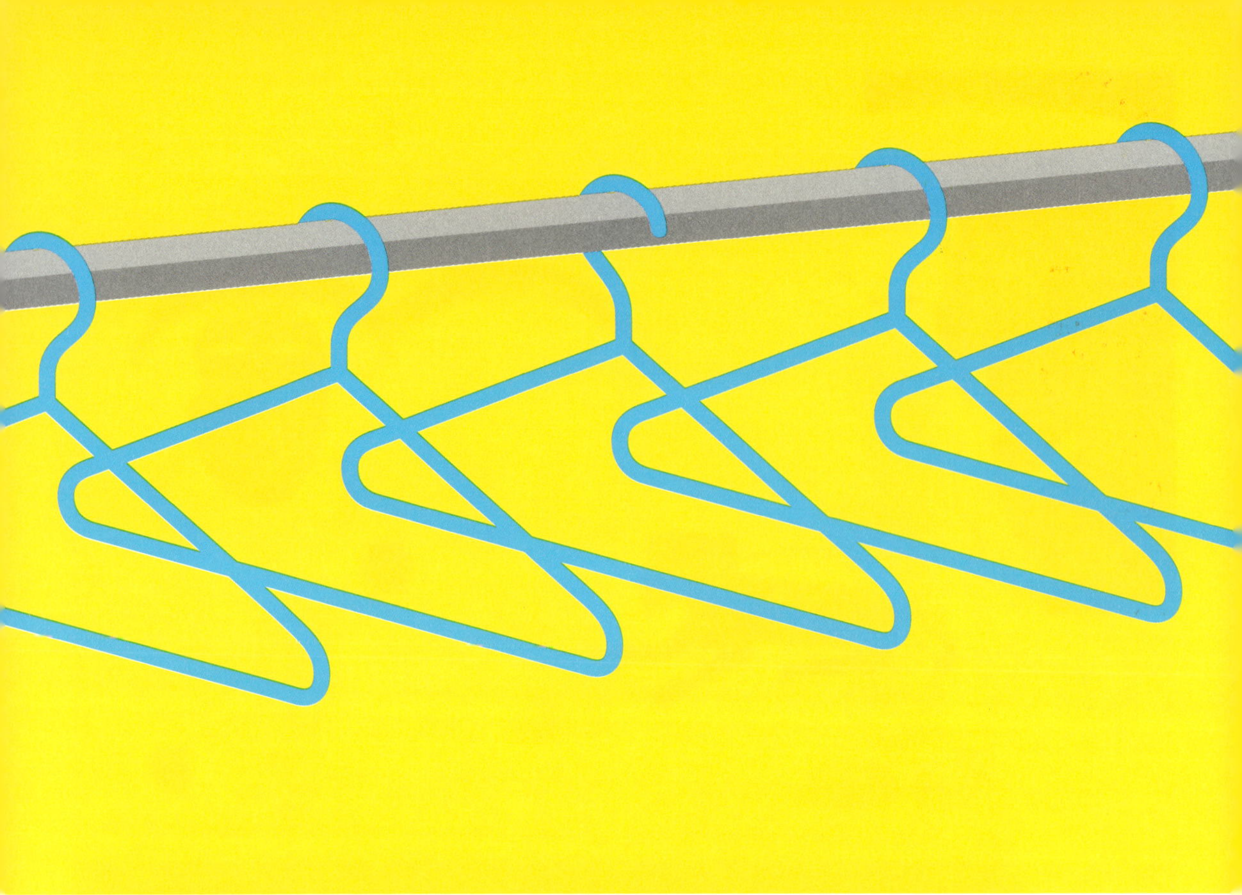

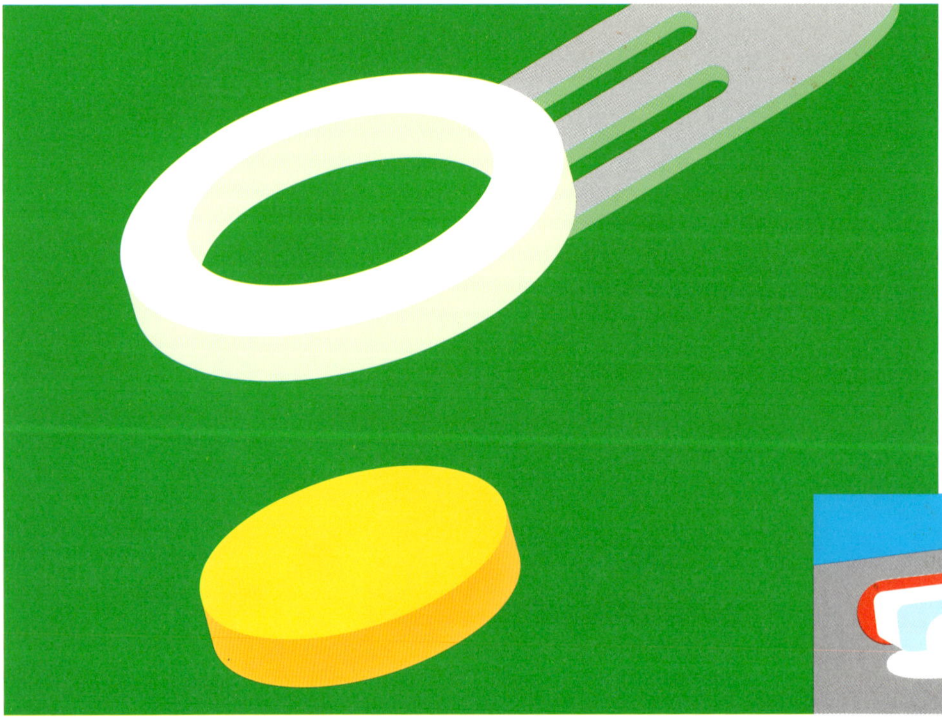

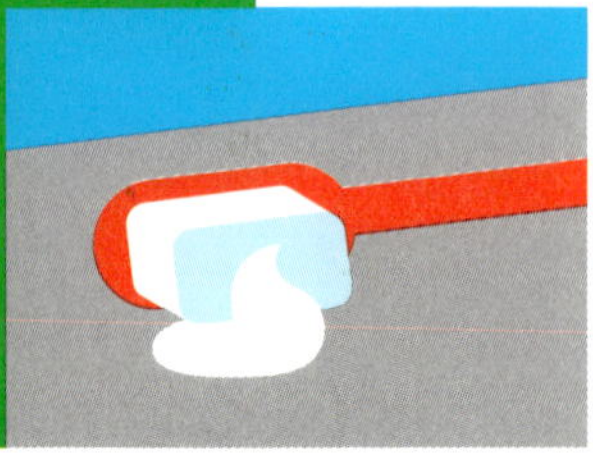

Original Works by Ryosuke Otomo

The illustrator creates this unique personal style using common shapes and colors. In this series, he captures common household items in a particular moment.

Illustrator: Ryosuke Otomo

Tips:

These expressive scene illustrations feature bold, saturated colors that add depth and dynamism to each artwork.

- C0 M0 Y100 K0
- C80 M0 Y0 K0

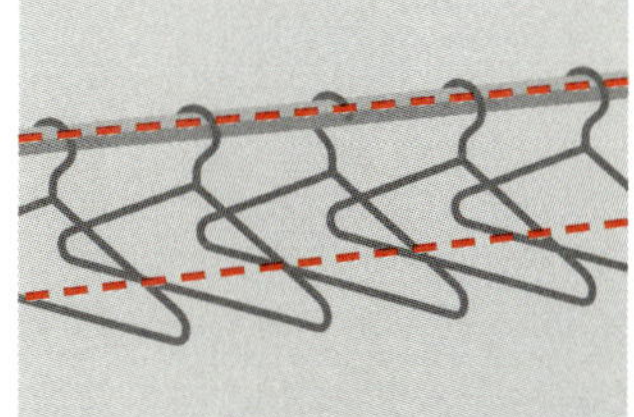

[特集]
TIME CAPSULE 2019
MetRO
miN.O
[メトロミニッツ]
11.20
2019NOV
SPECIAL
ISSUE

Time Capsule

This is the cover illustration for the magazine *Metro Minute*, distributed in Tokyo's subway. It celebrates the history of fashion building "PARCO" and the upcoming opening of PARCO Shibuya branch with the drawings of a couple lifting a time capsule.

Illustrator: Taro Uryu

Tips:

The illustrator uses PARCO's logo colors — red, green, and blue — for the illustration, with a background of large dots for a visually rich effect.

- C0 M100 Y100 K0
- C100 M0 Y100 K0
- C85 M50 Y0 K0
- *DIC621 85%

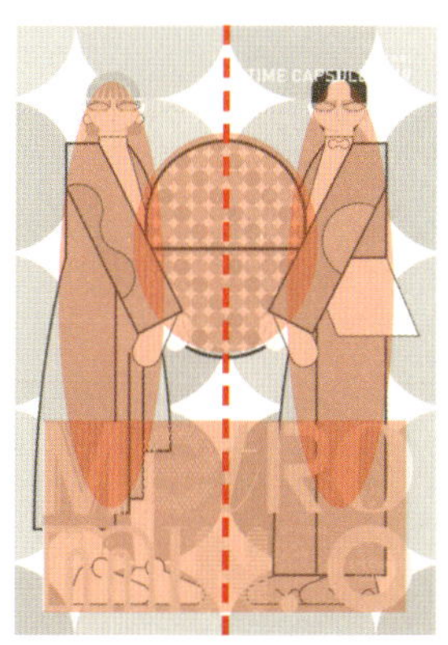

MATSURI

This artwork captures the joyful fusion of modernity and traditionality, music and dance, and the celebration of both genders at the 2021 Tokyo Art Festival.

Illustrator: Taro Uryu

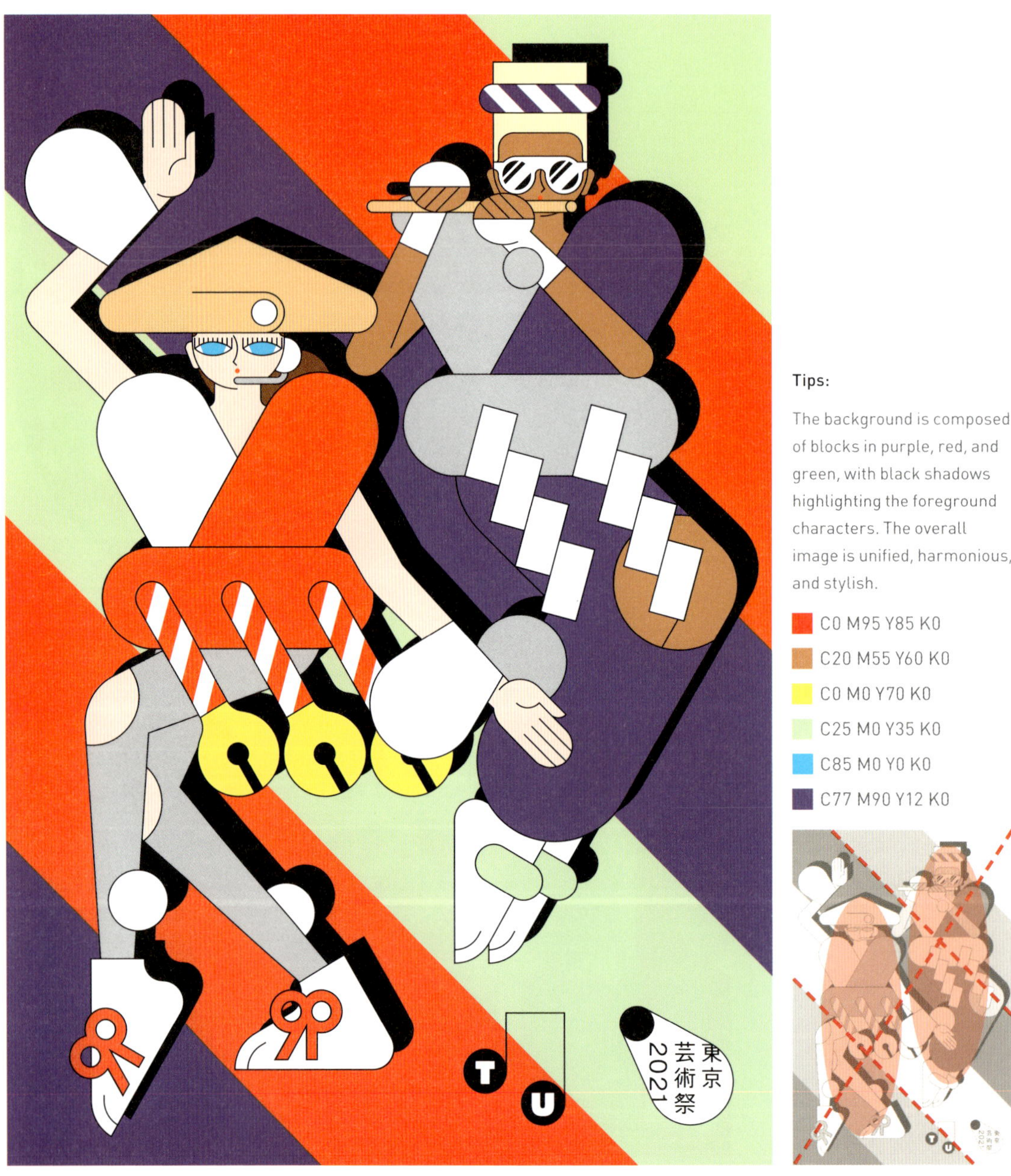

Tips:

The background is composed of blocks in purple, red, and green, with black shadows highlighting the foreground characters. The overall image is unified, harmonious, and stylish.

- C0 M95 Y85 K0
- C20 M55 Y60 K0
- C0 M0 Y70 K0
- C25 M0 Y35 K0
- C85 M0 Y0 K0
- C77 M90 Y12 K0

CRANE SUIT

This artwork is part of the "WAVE" exhibition's overseas expansion. The exhibition is held annually in Tokyo and features local Japanese artists. The overseas exhibition is touring in Los Angeles, São Paulo, and London. Inspired by the concept, the illustrator chose the crane, a famous Japanese migratory bird, as the main inspiration for this piece. He hopes it travels like the bird across the world.

Illustrator: Taro Uryu

Tips:

Simple lines and shapes can create stylish character designs.

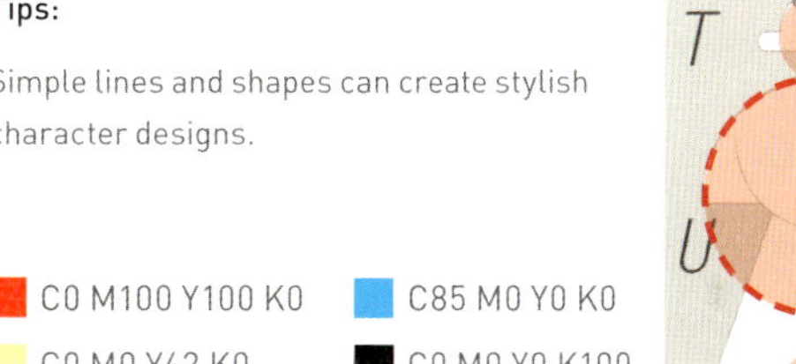

C0 M100 Y100 K0

C85 M0 Y0 K0

C0 M0 Y42 K0

C0 M0 Y0 K100

C0 M0 Y0 K30

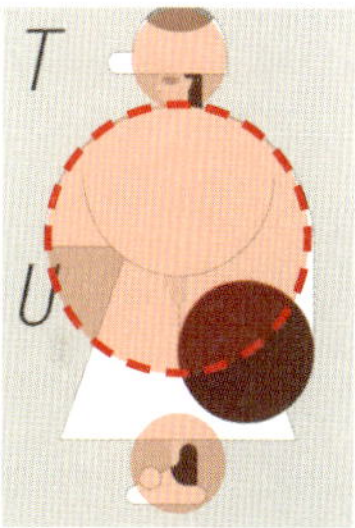

METROMIN.
【メトロミニッツ ローカリズム】
豊かな暮らしのヒントは「ローカルの日常」にある
LOCALRHYTHM
4.20 / MAY. 2022
233
特集
水のこと、考えてる？
METROMIN. LOCALRHYTHM
No.233
STARTS スターツ出版株式会社
あらかじめお伝えしておきますと、この特集では「どこの水がおいしい」とか、「1日に水をどれだけ飲むと健康になれる」とか、そういった話はいっさい出てきません。ガッカリさせてごめんなさい！　けれどこの4月に日本で初めて水道が民営化されるタイミングで、「水」のことを考えてほしいと思ったのです。とりわけ今回、メトロミニッツが注目したのが「雪どけ水」。東京に暮らす多くの人が「雪どけ水？　ナゼ？」と思うことでしょう。ですが雪は「天然のダム」。春から初夏にかけて「雪どけ水」があふれるから、田んぼに十分な水がいきわたり、秋においしいお米が穫れるのです。そもそも地球上の水は、雪と氷と水と水蒸気と…姿を変えながら循環しています。雪が山に降り積もり、あるべき季節にあるべき量の水が流れ出ることで、私たちの生活は調う――というわけで、今から美味、美景、暮らしと、「水」の恩恵を探す旅に出たいと思います。まずは「雪どけ水」がはぐくむ旬の味覚、いわば「雪どけ水グルメ」からお楽しみください！
水のこと、考えてる？
11
Illustration: TARO URYU
10

Tips:

The contrasting blue background and red lips create a captivating visual effect with sophisticated color clashes.

- C0 M100 Y80 K0
- C37 M0 Y0 K0
- C85 M45 Y0 K0
- *DIC621 85%

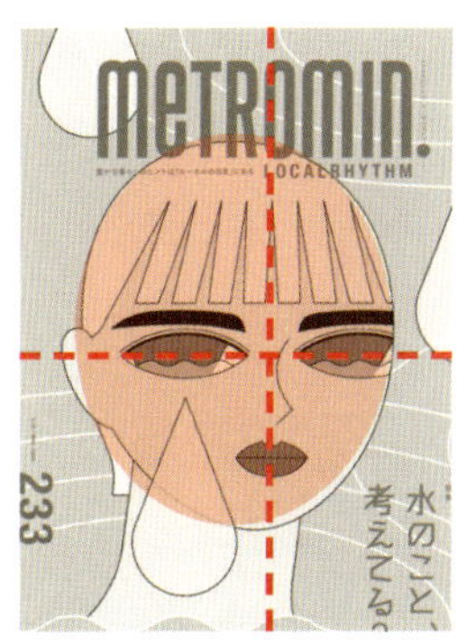

Woman Crying on The Water

Illustrator's cover for *Metro Minute* magazine features water theme with water colors and droplet-shaped elements.

Illustrator: Taro Uryu

第八十八凶
閑慮兩三
SUPER

Super Future

This is the designer's cassette tape cover design for a Japanese duo's album titled *Super Future*.

Designer: Josephine Grenier

Tips:

The designer utilized abstract and minimalist geometric shapes, along with bright and vibrant colors, to create a sense of "retro-futurism."

- C0 M100 Y100 K0
- C2 M32 Y0 K0
- C4 M3 Y77 K0
- C71 M0 Y54 K0
- C84 M15 Y73 K2
- C99 M0 Y0 K0

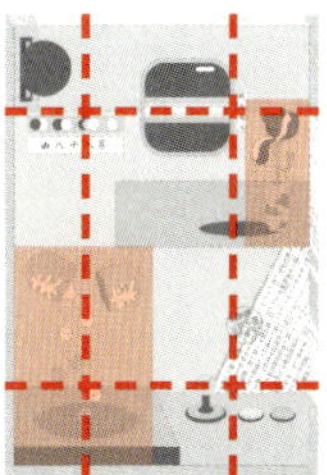

PLEASURE, NEUT

This illustration was created for the Japanese online magazine *Neut*, accompanying an article on desires during the global lockdown period (food, materialism, sexuality, knowledge, etc.).

Illustrator: Josephine Grenier

Tips:

Combining representative elements related to the theme and imagining their interactions and spatial relationships.

C0 M75 Y80 K0	C24 M42 Y55 K13
C5 M13 Y79 K0	C72 M0 Y68 K0
C7 M53 Y2 K0	C89 M36 Y79 K31
C76 M91 Y0 K0	C83 M62 Y2 K0

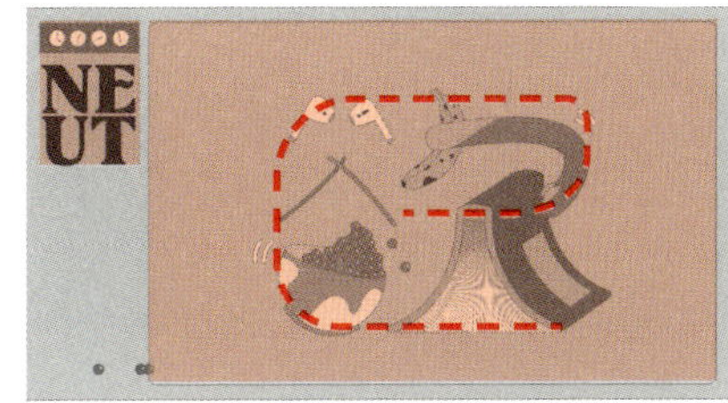

100-Years-Old Girl on The Moon

This series of illustrations was created for the group exhibition "I'M POSSIBLE," featuring Japanese graphic designers, held in Shanghai and Beijing. The concept behind the illustrations was inspired by the Windmill Festival in Okinawa, a celebration of longevity. The protagonist of the artworks is a 100-year-old girl floating on the moon's surface, symbolizing the connection between the possible and the impossible.

Illustrator: Taro Uryu

Tips:

The artworks embody the creative concept by skillfully combining shapes to form the central figure, resulting in a harmonious and distinctive aesthetic.

- C0 M100 Y100 K0
- C0 M13 Y13 K0
- C0 M5.5 Y10 K0
- C0 M5 Y30 K0
- C85 M0 Y0 K0
- C0 M0 Y0 K100

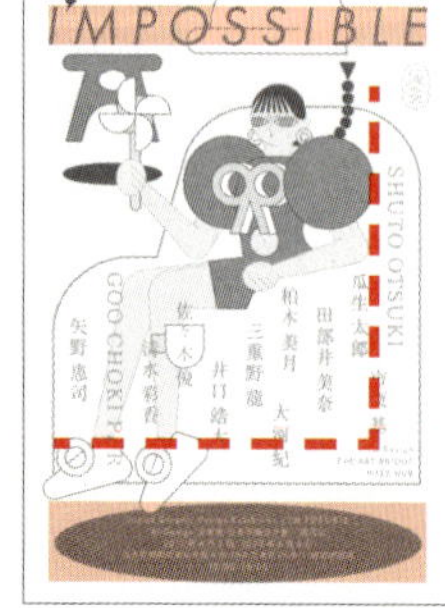

I'MPOSSIBLE

SHUTO OTSUKI
市東基
瓜生太郎
田部井美奈
柏木美月
大河紀
三重野龍
井口皓太
佐々木俊
清水彩香
GOO CHOKI PAR
矢野恵司

At Design
798 ART BRIDGE
PUSS HUB

Japan Graphic Design Exhibition - I'M POSSIBLE
At Design 企划展 日本平面设计展 - 我可以
2022 年 4 月 2 日 -2022 年 6 月 5 日
北京市朝阳区酒仙桥路 4 号 798 艺术区 D09-1 桥艺术空间
10:00-18:00

SoReWa Mata Betsu No Hanashi

Illustrator's solo exhibition showcased artworks titled "That's anotehr story."

Illustrator: fancomi

Client: Museum Shop T

Tips:

Several small paintings are combined together to form a larger artwork, showcasing an alternative composition technique worth learning.

- C0 M84 Y100 K0
- C0 M38 Y8 K0
- C3 M0 Y73 K0
- C27 M40 Y84 K4
- C78 M0 Y86 K0
- C0 M0 Y0 K40
- C73 M66 Y0 K0
- C100 M89 Y18 K5

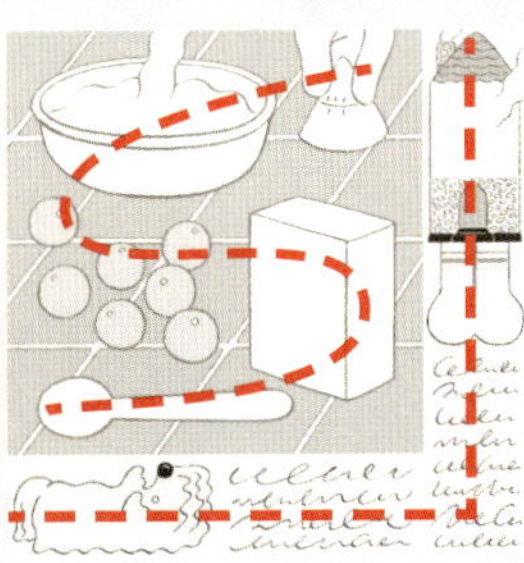

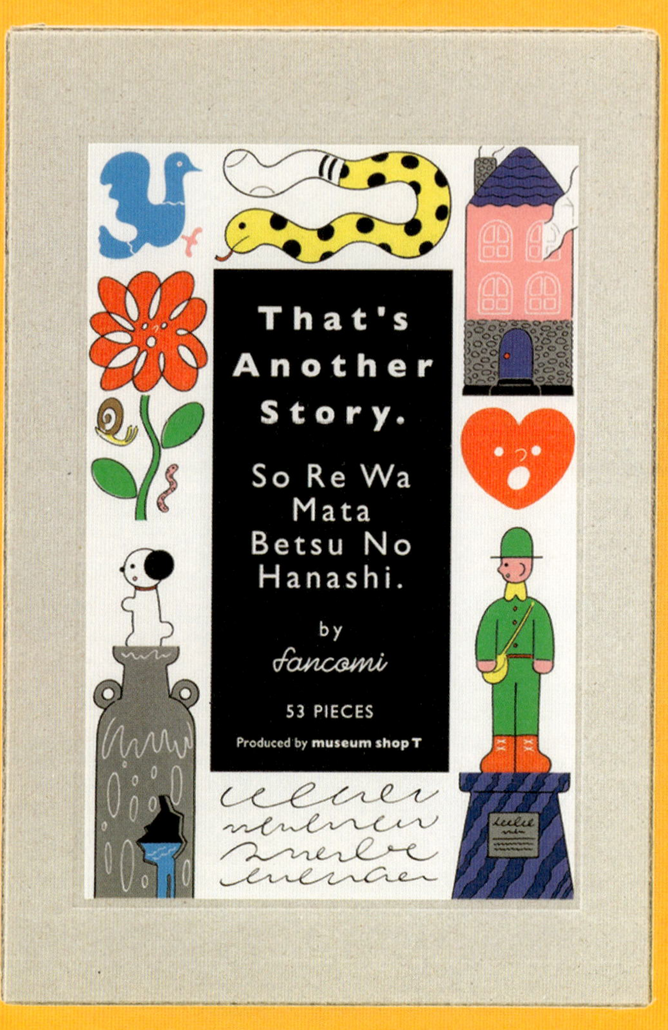

Tips:

The book cover uses a variety of small illustrations arranged around the visual center. This composition helps readers quickly grasp the content and directs their focus to the book title.

- C0 M84 Y100 K0
- C11 M35 Y21 K0
- C8 M4 Y63 K0
- C35 M42 Y77 K0
- C73 M15 Y81 K0
- C0 M0 Y0 K40
- C75 M67 Y13 K0
- C99 M85 Y25 K0

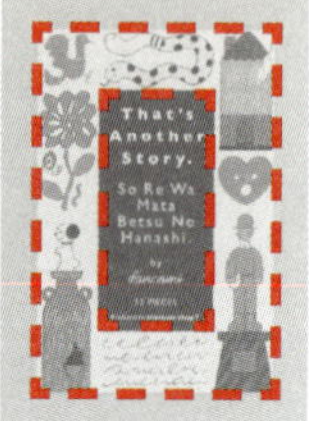

Tips:

Combining small pieces into a larger work helps readers recognize the illustrator's visual style and assists the illustrator in establishing their unique visual language.

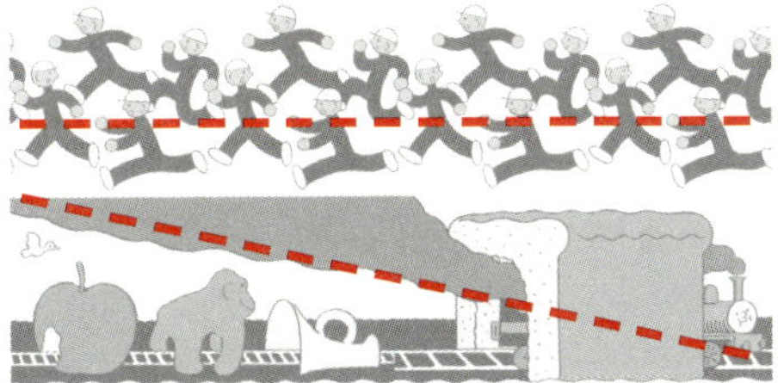

Nihonbashi Bridge

Those illustrations were supplied for an exhibition by local companies in Nihonbashi, Japan, showcasing the collaborative efforts for sustainable development since the Edo period.

Illustrator: Atsushi Hirano

Design Studio: AFFORDANCE inc.

Planning and Management: CreativeOut Inc.

Main Organizers: Mitsui Fudosan, Nihonbashi Area Management

Tips:

The main visual is based on a Möbius strip, with various characters added by the illustrator, symbolizing "loop" and sustainable development.

- C4 M0 Y94 K0
- C0 M40 Y0 K0
- C2 M88 Y69 K0
- C79 M3 Y92 K0
- C72 M30 Y0 K0
- C0 M0 Y0 K100

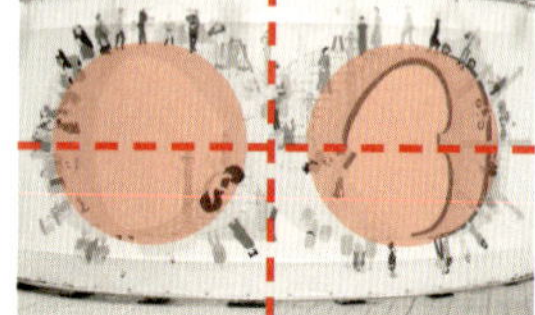

Cookie Union

Designed for the packaging of the cookie brand Cookie Union.

Illustrator: Atsushi Hirano

Design Studio: AFFORDANCE inc.

Tips: The illustrator uses "continuous quadrants" for an infinite composition. Vibrant colors and playful graphics make the artwork lively, boosting brand recognition.

- C4 M99 Y99 K0
- C9 M1 Y56 K0
- C10 M0 Y92 K0
- C28 M48 Y83 K8
- C45 M64 Y76 K43
- C67 M22 Y47 K2
- C96 M10 Y94 K1
- C45 M3 Y0 K0
- C99 M93 Y6 K2
- C42 M86 Y1 K0

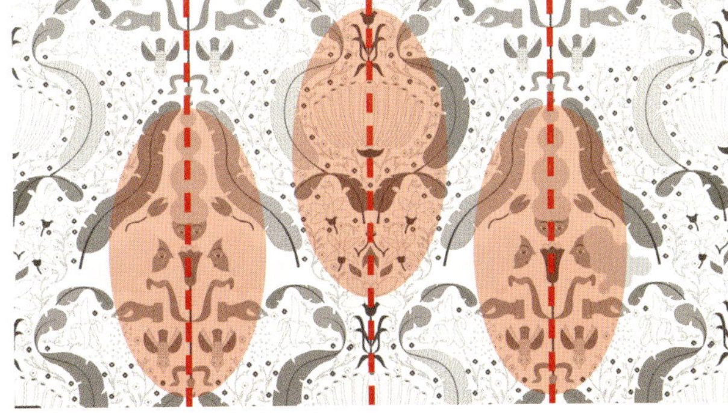

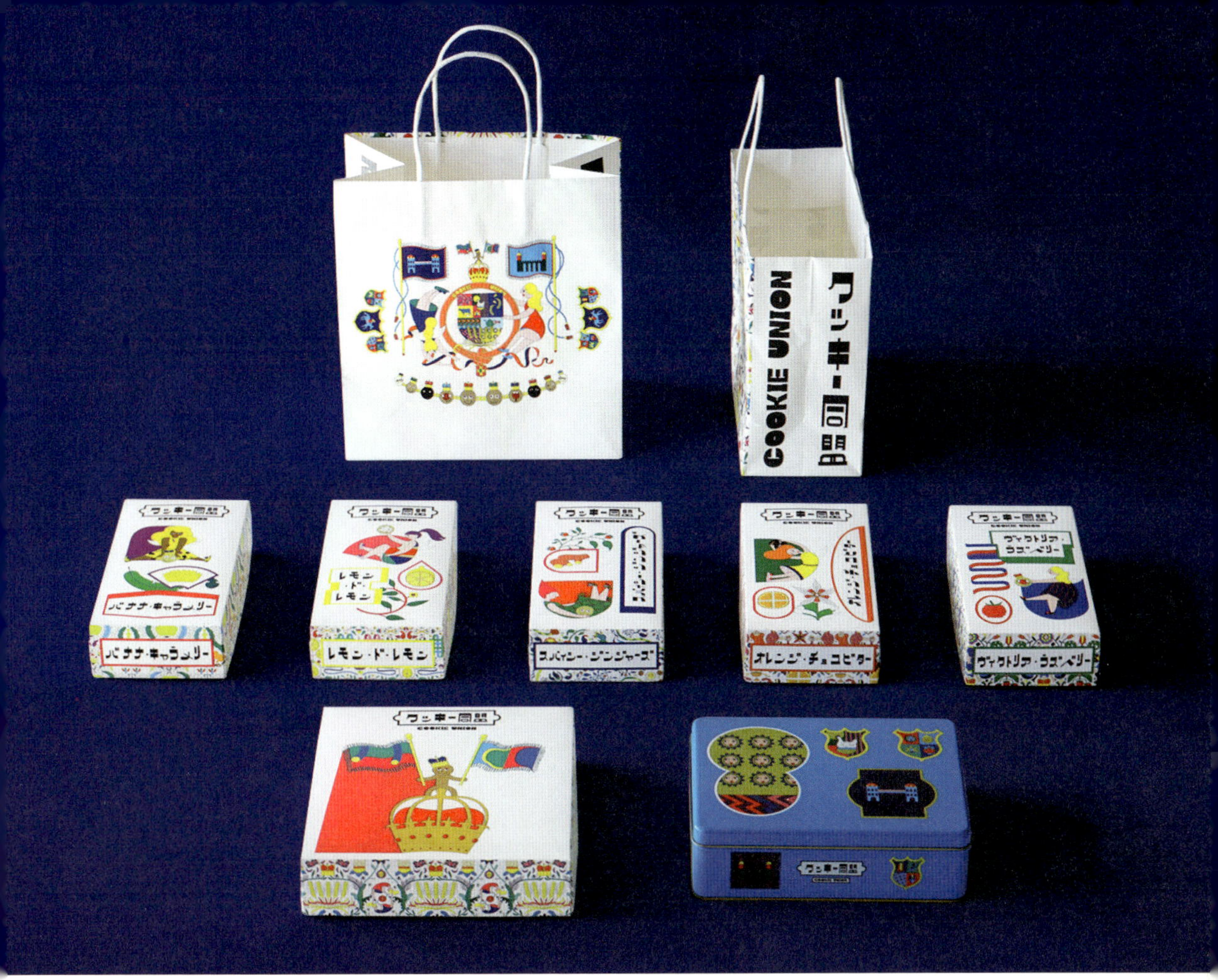

クッキー同盟
COOKIE UNION
ヴィクトリア・ラズベリー
ヴィクトリア・ラズベリー

見てジリジリ、試してメキメキの展覧会
IAMAS ARTIST FILE #06
クワクボリョウタ
会田大也
KUWAKUBO RYOTA AIDA DAIYA
みる
こころみる
LOOK AT, LOOK INTO, LOOK BACK
かえりみる
高校生以下は
観覧無料!
2018.9.8［土］—11.3［土・祝］
岐阜県美術館 開館時間 10:00–18:00（入場は17:30まで）
夜間開館日 9月21日（金）、10月19日（金）は20:00まで開館（入場は19:30まで）
休館日 月曜日（祝・休日の場合は翌平日）
観覧料 一般 500円（400円） 大学生 300円（250円） 高校生以下は無料
※（ ）内は20名以上の団体割引料金
※身体障がい者手帳、療育手帳、精神障がい者保健福祉手帳の交付を受けている方およびその付き添いの方（1名まで）は観覧無料
IAMAS
岐阜県美術館
THE MUSEUM OF FINE ARTS, GIFU
主催：岐阜県美術館、情報科学芸術大学院大学［IAMAS］｜共催：岐阜新聞社 岐阜放送
後援：岐阜県教育委員会、岐阜市教育委員会、大垣市教育委員会
協力：岐阜県社会保険協会｜制作：IAMAS あたらしいTOYプロジェクト
Illustration: fancomi

LOOK AT, LOOK INTO, LOOK BACK

This is the main visual created by the illustrator for the exhibition "LOOK AT, LOOK INTO, LOOK BACK."

Illustrator: fancomi

Designer Studio: STUDIO PT.

Client: THE MUSEUM OF FINE ARTS, GIFU

Tips:

The color scheme is minimalistic, and the poster is composed of multiple small scenes.

- C0 M40 Y60 K0
- C0 M10 Y70 K0
- C50 M0 Y20 K0
- C40 M0 Y90 K0

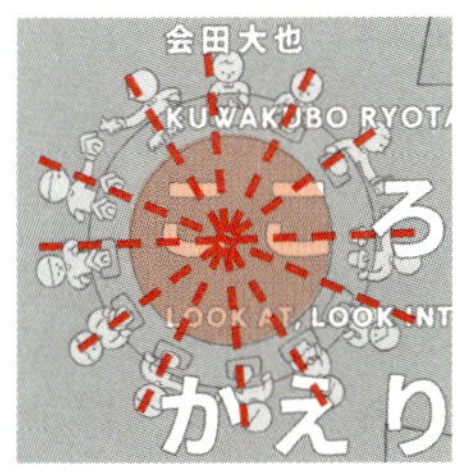

Step with Slippers, Art Rink in Yokohama Red Brick Warehouse

Illustrators unpis and Moeno Otsu created a 100-meter-long mural displayed on temporary walls at the Yokohama Red Brick Warehouse Skating Rink. With the theme of "Dancing With Furniture And Household Items" and the concept of "wearing slippers," they depicted heartwarming scenes during the COVID-19 pandemic.

Illustrators: unpis, Moeno Otsu

Tips: The long canvas cleverly connects each scene, while the abundant wavy lines add a sense of dynamism.

C0 M83 Y98 K0	C25 M36 Y68 K2
C1 M16 Y55 K0	C62 M28 Y62 K2
C2 M3 Y64 K0	C76 M35 Y0 K0

nezumi
neko
kitsune
imo
mushi
tanuki
kame
saru
oni

NIHON HAKU Postcard Book *The Circle of Japanese Culture*

This is an illustration created by the designer with the theme of "maru" (means circle in Japanese), incorporating elements from Japanese folk tales and traditional musical instruments.

Illustrator: fancomi
Client: Agency for Cultural Affairs
Project Planning: CINRA, inc.

Tips:

The circular drum is positioned at the center of the composition, with other traditional figures surrounding in a balanced and evenly distributed manner.

C0 M100 Y100 K0	C75 M0 Y80 K0
C0 M0 Y70 K0	C100 M80 Y0 K20
C35 M45 Y75 K0	C70 M60 Y0 K0

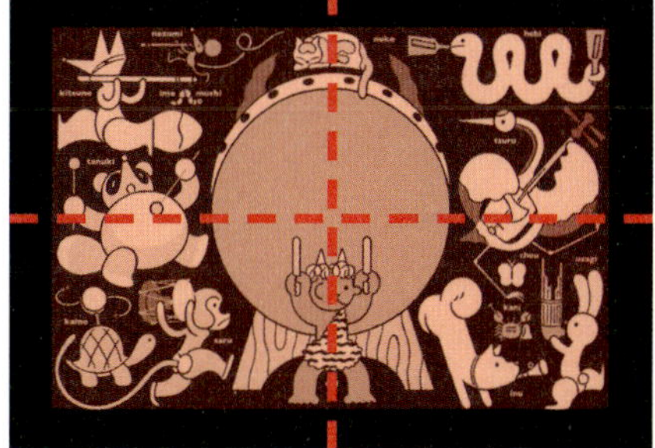

Unknown Object

The illustrator creatively recombines various everyday objects, offering a fresh perspective on ordinary items.

Illustrator: unpis

Tips:

The diagonal composition adds a playful touch to the artwork.

- C0 M88 Y97 K0
- C0 M70 Y36 K0
- C0 M30 Y93 K0
- C2 M15 Y55 K0
- C2 M0 Y37 K0
- C14 M0 Y16 K0
- C47 M5 Y37 K0

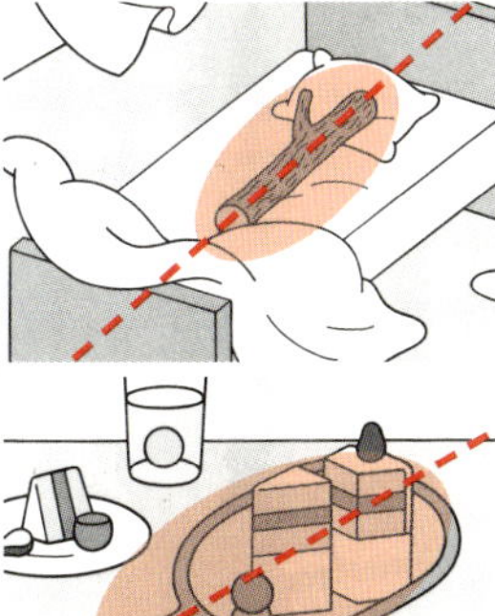

THE NORTH FACE

The illustrator created nature-themed illustrations for THE NORTH FACE brand, highlighting the connection between our daily diet and the natural environment.

Illustrator: unpis
Designer: Masaki Yato
Editorial Director: Eri Ishida

私たちの日々の食事は、
アウトドアフィールドと
つながっている

Tips: Each illustration has its own theme, portraying the concept of a low-carbon diet.

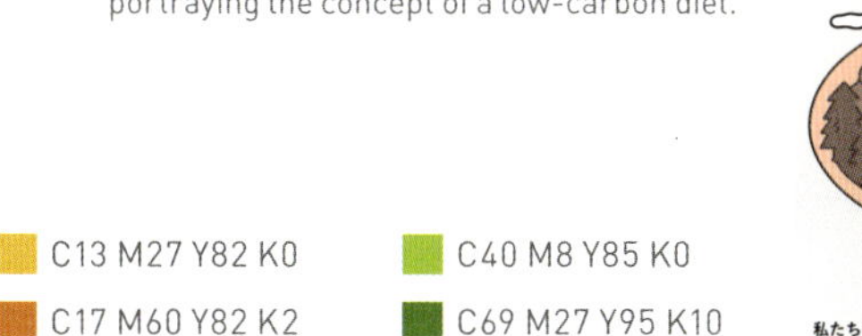

- C13 M27 Y82 K0
- C17 M60 Y82 K2
- C33 M72 Y87 K29
- C40 M8 Y85 K0
- C69 M27 Y95 K10
- C73 M38 Y92 K29

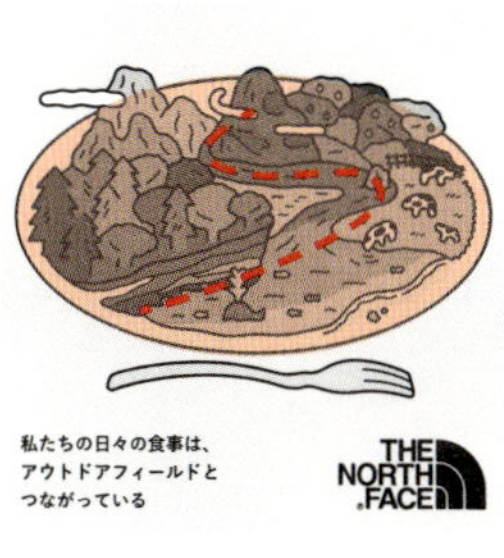

私たちの日々の食事は、
アウトドアフィールドと
つながっている

THE NORTH FACE

Original Works by Kosamesoda

Inspired by the illustrator's daily life, the unique style showcases the tranquil moments in everyday dining.

Illustrator: Kosamesoda

Tips:

These artworks feature everyday dining as their theme, with consistent composition and balanced elements. The use of color blocks divides the background, creating a harmonious contrast with the food and conveying a fresh and lively feeling.

- C0 M80 Y0 K0
- C0 M30 Y0 K0
- C3 M36 Y43 K0
- C4 M6 Y86 K0
- C53 M0 Y76 K0
- C91 M0 Y67 K0
- C61 M0 Y15 K0
- C87 M55 Y0 K0

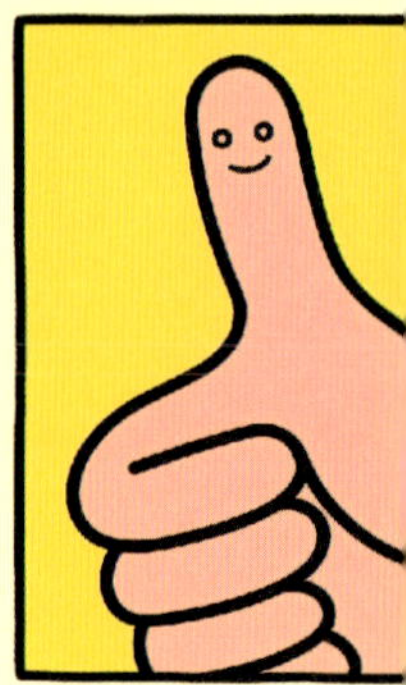

NONIO

This is a packaging illustration exclusively designed for the Japanese market, showcasing NONIO's reusable bottle for replenishable mouthwash.

Illustrator: unpis

Art Director: Dai Goto

Designer: Rieko Hidaka

Client: Lion Corporation

Tips:

The lines are clear and powerful, yet soft, showing a relaxed and lively atmosphere.

C22 M0 Y53 K0

C1 M1 Y24 K0

C2 M6 Y86 K0

C55 M13 Y85 K1

C38 M0 Y1 K0

C84 M36 Y13 K0

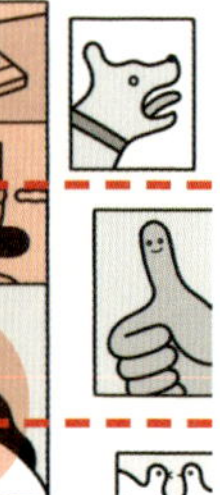

Works by Megumi Yamazaki

The illustrator's artwork is rich in color and full of childlike charm, showcasing their whimsical imagination from everyday life.

Illustrator: Megumi Yamazaki

My Homies

Tips:

The illustrator employed a "mandala" composition style, adding richness and interest to the artworks. Watercolor and colored pencils were used to create texture and depth.

C0 M99 Y54 K0
C0 M73 Y60 K0
C44 M55 Y0 K0
C6 M3 Y74 K0
C0 M40 Y82 K0
C43 M0 Y92 K0
C96 M60 Y48 K5
C58 M0 Y18 K0
C0 M0 Y0 K20

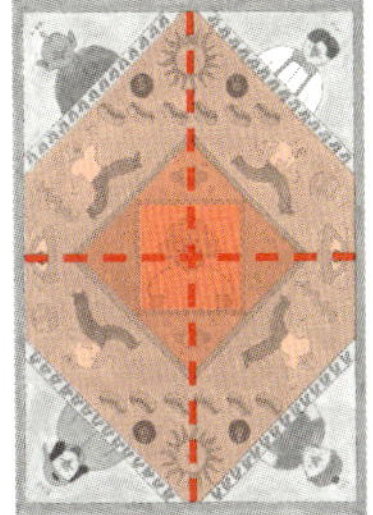

Tips:

The illustrator cartoonizes the characters, animals and plants, and is good at using different shades of blue to create depth in the picture, as well as creating a deep, mysterious atmosphere.

- C0 M40 Y80 K0
- C55 M10 Y15 K0
- C90 M60 Y35 K0
- C40 M40 Y40 K100

Works by NAMISATORI

The illustrator specializes in depicting strange plants and creatures that exist in his "brain greenhouse." Inspired by literature, music, and nature, his artworks embody contradictory concepts of unsettling comfort and adorable yet mischievous beings.

Illustrator: NAMISATORI

A GOOD DAY
TO DIE...

REST
IN
ENTER

Works by Momoko Nakamura

❶ This work serves as the main visual for the illustrator's personal exhibition, titled "Diary," and it is also a part of her actual diary. ❷ – ❸ Visual design for LUMINE's 2021 Christmas advertisement. The illustrator portrays "personal thoughts" as "flowers of sound," and showcases a woman's thoughts sprout from her mouth and blossom into flowers.

Illustrator: Momoko Nakamura

❶

Tips:

The diagonal composition, combined with Christmas colors and elements, enriches the artwork.

- C42 M98 Y100 K8
- C7 M56 Y65 K0
- C3 M25 Y20 K0
- C16 M14 Y89 K0
- C45 M5 Y68 K0
- C85 M56 Y91 K25
- C73 M24 Y48 K0
- C80 M56 Y7 K0

❷

The painting features a refined gray palette, conveying simplicity and elegance. The man embodies the earth, while the woman tenderly kisses him, showcasing a distinct intimacy.

- C0 M22 Y6 K0
- C37 M60 Y79 K0
- C69 M18 Y59 K0
- C74 M63 Y44 K2

❸

Fragments

Amidst travel restrictions caused by the COVID-19 pandemic, the illustrator portrays street scenes of cities like San Francisco, Paris, and Chihuahua. She captures the fleeting "fragments" of these cities using her distinct painting style. By employing a simplified brushstroke, the figures on the roadside are subtly blurred, highlighting the beauty that arises from their ambiguous presence.

Illustrator: Nao Tatsumi

Tips:

The illustrator skillfully combines soft colors, delicate brushstrokes, and vibrant color blocks, creating rich and dimensional artworks with a tranquil and harmonious atmosphere.

- C21 M100 Y65 K0
- C0 M18 Y95 K0
- C29 M11 Y2 K0
- C98 M70 Y0 K0

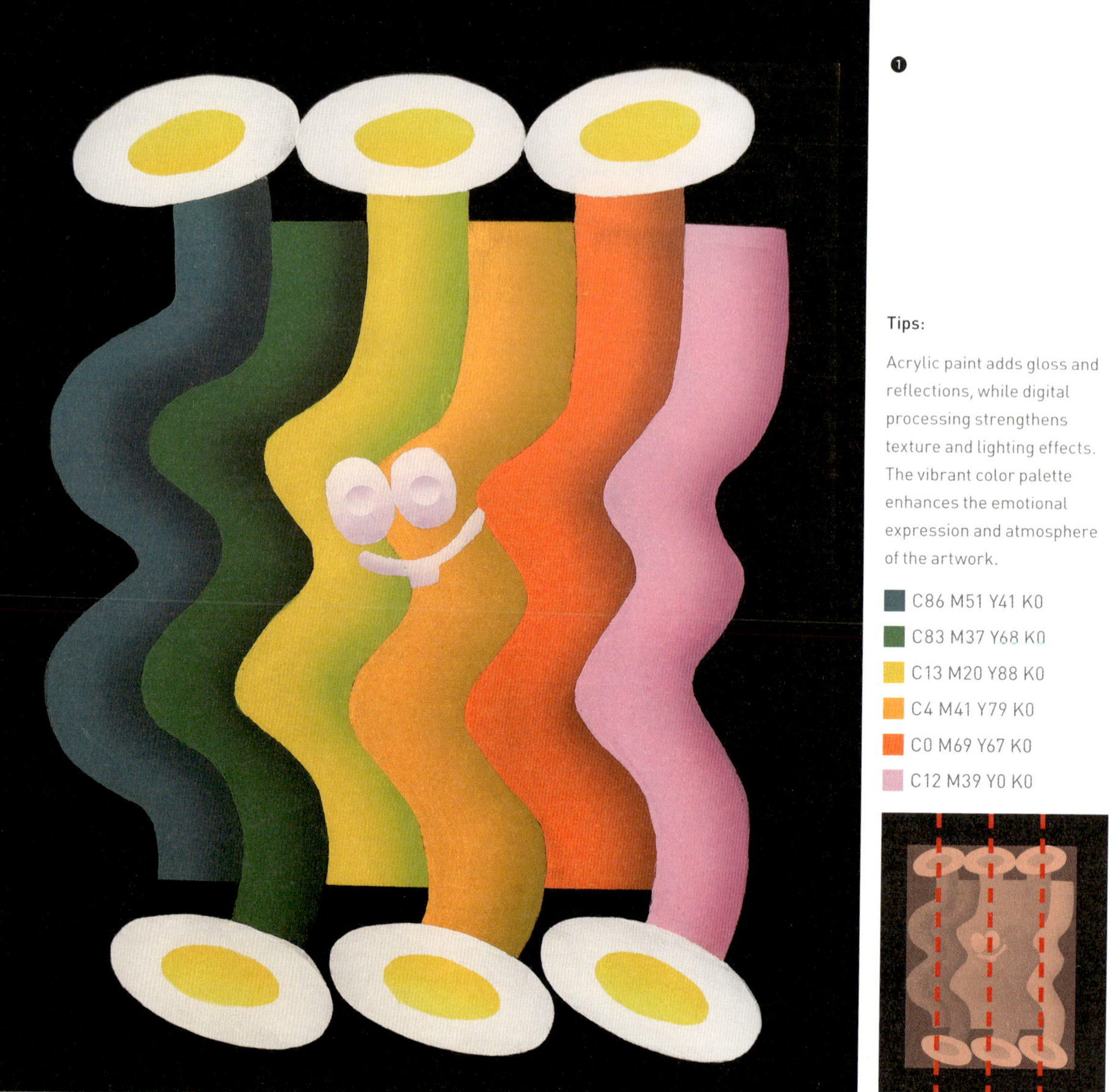

❶

Tips:

Acrylic paint adds gloss and reflections, while digital processing strengthens texture and lighting effects. The vibrant color palette enhances the emotional expression and atmosphere of the artwork.

- C86 M51 Y41 K0
- C83 M37 Y68 K0
- C13 M20 Y88 K0
- C4 M41 Y79 K0
- C0 M69 Y67 K0
- C12 M39 Y0 K0

Works by Chieko Kogure

❶ Personal work, Acrylic On Canvas. ❷ On The Cube, and On The Orb, 2022, Acrylic On Paper. ❸ On The Wave, and On The Crystal, Acrylic On paper.

Illustrator: Chieko Kogure

CHIEKO KOGURE
EXHIBITION
2019 JAN, 16th - MAR, 17th
at ORBIT
SANGENCYAYA, TOKYO

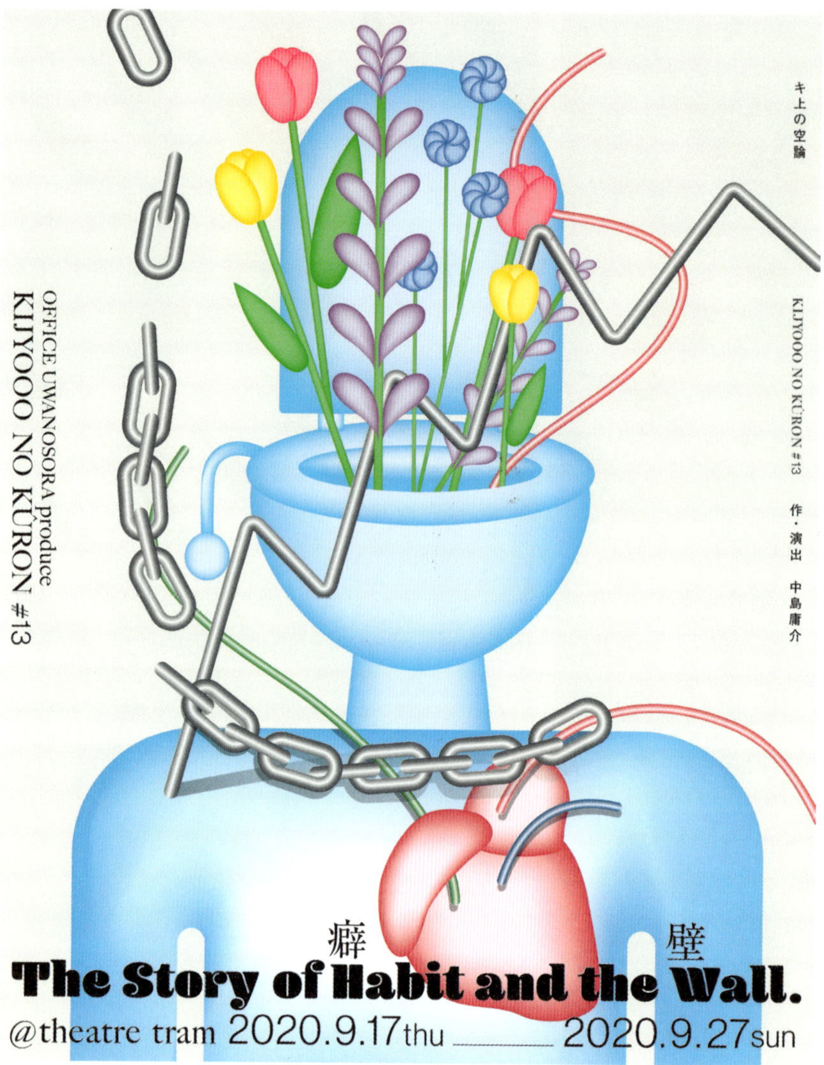

KIJYOOO NO KÛRON #13

The artwork depicts the story of "Habit" and "Wall," designed for a stage play poster. It explores the connection between human habits and dividing walls. In Japanese, habit and wall both sound "heki." The message is that human "obsessions" should break free from constraints, symbolized by "wall," and express themselves boldly, just like a toilet transforming into a flowerpot.

Designer: Maiko Higuchi

キ上の空論

KIJYOOO NO KŪRON #13

作・演出　中島庸介

癖　壁

The Story of Habit and the Wall.

@theatre tram 2020.9.17thu ——— 2020.9.27sun

Tips:

Vibrant shadows enhance the three-dimensional effect, while the popular color palette and technique contribute to the contemporary style. This innovative artwork effectively enriches and emphasizes the theme.

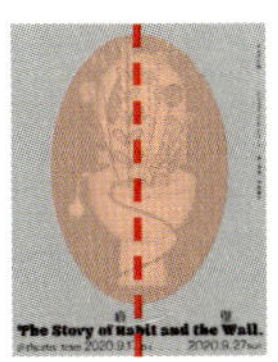

Nectar

The illustrator depicts a cherished childhood memory of savoring the nectar of roadside flowers with friends on the way home from school, from a unique perspective.

Illustrator: Yuta Miura

Tips:

Placing vibrant orange flowers at the center, contrasting with the gray background, and using a mesh barrier for depth, the artwork achieves a layered composition.

- C0 M80 Y85 K0
- C76 M2 Y84 K0
- C0 M0 Y0 K45
- C0 M0 Y0 K100

Stranger

The blurred face of a stranger in a dream has been abstracted by the illustrator into the shape of a flower, exuding a romantic beauty and imaginative charm.

Illustrator: Yuta Miura

Tips:

Using varying sizes of intersecting and tangent ellipses, the illustrator creates a clever representation of flower petals.

- C5 M100 Y96 K1
- C99 M98 Y14 K10
- C53 M0 Y11 K0

LANDING

The illustrator created a series of artworks based on the term "Landing," representing the relationship and movement between fish and nets in the sea during fishing.

Illustrator: Yuta Miura

Tips:

The fishing tools and lively fish are expressed in contrasting orange and blue, with soft curves depicting the flexibility of the nets and the agility of the fish.

- C0 M50 Y84 K0
- C87 M50 Y46 K0

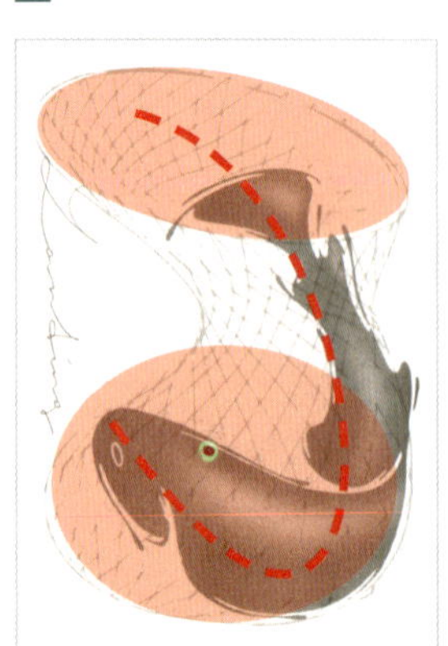

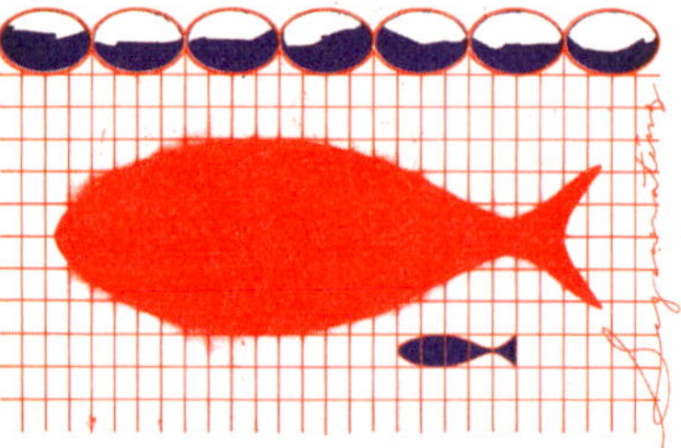

Entangling
Releasing

A Series of Single-Picture Stories Formed by Mysterious Grit

This illustrator crafts captivating and imaginative stories on a single sheet, incorporating unique shapes and textured elements.

Illustrator: Yosuke Kinoshita

Tips:

When creating illustrations, breaking free from boundaries and using comic-style panels can form a larger interconnected artwork.

C1 M78 Y96 K4	C60 M15 Y21 K2	C84 M35 Y64 K36
C11 M34 Y89 K16	C79 M43 Y0 K0	C0 M0 Y0 K100

Chapter 5

JAPANESE ILLUSTRATION

Second printing of the first edition, May 2025

sendpoints

PUBLISHED BY SendPoints Publishing Co., Ltd.
ADDRESS: Unit 23, L1/F Mirror Tower, 61 Mody Road, Tsim Sha Tsui, Kowloon, Hong Kong, China
PUBLISHER: Lin Gengli
CHIEF EDITOR: Wu Dongyan
DEVELOPMENT EDITOR: Wu Dongyan
EXECUTIVE EDITOR: Liang Xinyi
COVER ILLUSTRATOR: Agata Yamaguchi (JP)
EXECUTIVE ART EDITOR: Zhang Zichen
TRANSLATORS: Pan Yingzhao, Liang Xinyi
PROOFREADING: Liang Xinyi, Li Jia, Huang Chujun

SALES DIRECTOR: Philip Tsang
TEL: +852 6296 2246
EMAIL: sales@sppub.com
WEBSITE: www.sppub.com

ISBN 978-988-76791-7-2

Printed and bound in China.

Facebook

Instagram

X

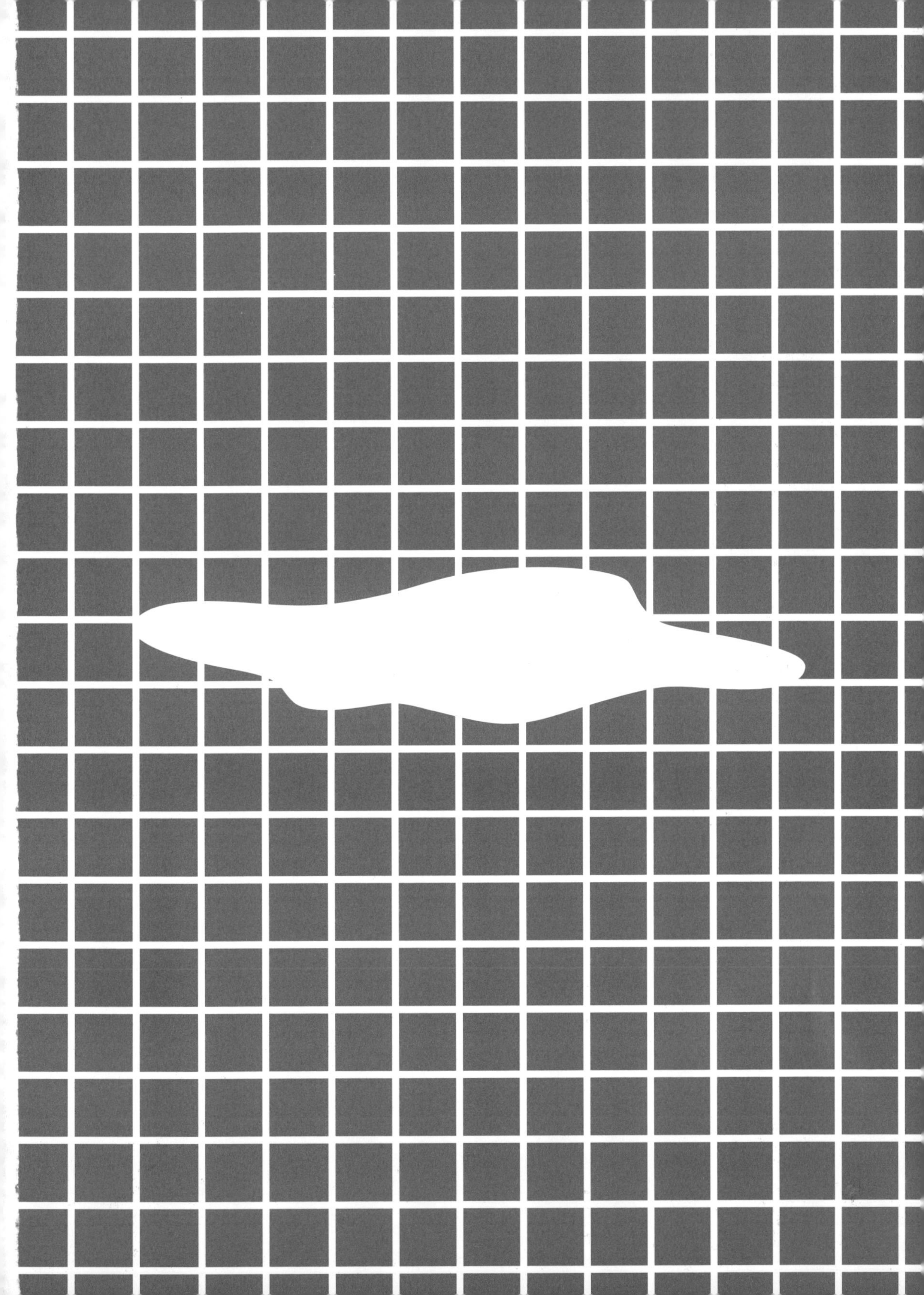

ACKNOWLEDGEMENTS

We would like to thank all the designers and contributors who have been involved in the production of this book; their contributions have been indispensable to its creation. We would also like to express our gratitude to all the producers for their invaluable opinions and assistance throughout this project. And to the many others whose names are not credited but have made specific input in this book, we thank you for your continuous support.

FUTURE COOPERATIONS

If you wish to participate in SendPoints' future projects and publications, please send your website or portfolio to editor02@sendpoints.cn